St. Tom's Cathedral

There is something magnificent about discovering a true-life passion, and there is something unparalleled about the ability to craft words and stories to share that passion with others. This is the brilliance of Bryan Hendricks's *St. Tom's Cathedral.* It is a book that invites readers to the intimacy of a hunter's devotion. It is not merely another book about hunting; it is a book of reverence and veneration, a benediction upon the art and aesthetic of the hunt and the object of the hunt. It is a tribute and parable, a collection of memoirs that honor the majesty of the noble turkey and celebrate the virtue of family and friendship. Hendricks's *St. Tom's Cathedral* will sit on the dais alongside turkey books by the likes of Tom Kelly, Henry Edwards Davis, Archibald Rutledge, and Gene Nunnery. It is, frankly, a remarkable read.

—SID DOBRIN, Professor and Chair,
Department of English, University of Florida
Author of *Distance Casting: Words and Ways of the Saltwater Fishing Life*
and *Fishing, Gone?: Saving the Ocean through Sportfishing*

If *St. Tom's Cathedral* does anything, it places author Bryan Hendricks at the top of a list of the nation's finest outdoor writers. No. Make that *writers*, period.

—DAN KIBLER, Editor, *Carolina Sportsman Magazine*

Like an American Sherpa, Hendricks escorts readers into the rolling hills, woodlots, and fields of the central U.S. to outwit the cagiest animal on the continent. Though unique to his experience, Hendricks's anecdotes are relatable to anyone who's pursued Benjamin Franklin's favorite bird. Read *St. Tom's Cathedral,* and you'll laugh, learn, and be thoroughly entertained. It's an instant classic that grizzled veterans of the sport will pass to their prodigy with admonitions to pore over its pages before ever stepping boot in the spring woods.

—**TODD MASSON,** host of the *Marsh Man Masson* YouTube channel

St. Tom's Cathedral

Bryan L. Hendricks

St. Tom's Cathedral: A Turkey Hunter's Quest for His Best
Bryan Hendricks

Copyright © 2022

Published by Big B Publishing
401 Hill Rd., Malvern, AR 72104
(501) 831-6801
bryan.hendricks860@gmail.com

ISBN: 978-1-7373990-0-1 (paperback), 978-1-7373990-1-8 (hardback),
          978-1-7373990-2-5 (epub), 978-1-7373990-3-2 (audiobook)

Editor: Jen Para
Publishing and Design Services: MelindaMartin.me
Cover Art: Ginger Martin

St. Tom's Cathedral

A Turkey Hunter's Quest for His Best

A MEMOIR

Bryan L. Hendricks

FOREWORD

When Bryan told me that he was working on a turkey hunting novel, of course it piqued my interest. Anything "turkey" will stop me dead in my tracks, and usually any level of turkey talk will send me into fits of natural-voice owl hooting and hen yelping. It comes straight from my soul—a soul that's fueled by the King of Spring.

Admittedly, Bryan's nonchalant mention of this in-the-works novel triggered initial skepticism. In a day when self-publishing is easier than ever, anyone can come to the table with "the next big thing."

Now, try to produce a contemporary novel about turkey hunting that's worth a damn, and that might be more challenging than breaking a strutter from his harem. But in Bryan's case, I should've known he would scratch out a fresh call to the Tenth Legion that resonates beyond measure. Combine an award-winning veteran journalist with his religious passion for gobblers and a masterful storytelling ability, and the result is a holy scripture that turkey hunters will revisit annually to prepare for their spring pilgrimage.

Even bolder to me than birthing a meaningful novel about turkey hunting is why Bryan would ever dream of asking me to write its foreword. On the surface, we're merely acquaintances who brushed elbows in a media deer camp at Cottonmouth—the legendary property where Will Primos and his crew have made endless hunting TV magic. However, after spending a few days together, it was clear we had a bond that only hunters can understand. Our rapport was sealed in blood when we discovered our mutual core affliction: turkeys. In the pages to follow, it becomes even easier to understand why Bryan deemed me worthy of ushering you into St. Tom's Cathedral. He radiates a genuine reverence for the unique characters he's stumbled across throughout his outdoor journeys. Apparently, I was blessed to make the cut.

Like Bryan, the wild turkey has become a defining force in my existence. As he writes, "Spring's scent is that of newborn nature. Like line-dried laundry, it wafts renewal and hope." Some of the finest people, best experiences, and greatest lessons have landed in my lap thanks to a career that has involved chasing all of the North American turkey subspecies.

There are spectators, and there are visionaries. Turkey hunting can transform you into the latter. To become a consistently successful turkey hunter, you must learn to appreciate and analyze all the small details in the architecture of *St. Tom's Cathedral*. Only then will you see the full picture, discover what's important, and get an edge.

As Bryan vividly conveys in the pages to follow, this visionary lens of a seasoned turkey hunter transcends into every aspect of life. How we stand up to challenges, deal with conflicts, get our egos in check, value life, or face death and grief—all can be taught through our pursuit of the wild turkey.

Step into *St. Tom's Cathedral* and receive his communion.

—Josh Dahlke
Feb. 17, 2021

PROLOGUE

On Feb. 23, 2009, I was diagnosed with advanced stage III rectal cancer.

The day was a maelstrom of emotional body blows in which my oncologist, surgical oncologist, and radiologist explained the details of my imminent demise. It's like listening to your mechanic describe the procedure to rebuild your worn-out transmission.

"We're going to replace your seals and bearings. Your spider gear is stripped, and we'll have to replace your torque converter."

The difference is that with cancer treatment, you don't get a cost estimate or a warranty. You send the jalopy to the shop irrespective of cost. Even if your mechanic completes the repair, there's no guarantee the old heap will run again.

My treatment would begin with six weeks of chemotherapy concurrent with twenty-five radiation treatments, five days a week for five weeks. After a short recovery period, most of my terminal plumbing would be removed, and I would be given a temporary colostomy. Afterward, the colostomy would be taken down and my colon reopened. I would then endure about six more months of chemotherapy. If all went well, I might live.

For my chemotherapy infusions, an intravenous port would be surgically implanted in my shoulder. My wife, Laura, and my sweet sister-in-law Mary dabbed away tears as my oncologist described the procedure.

"Does it matter which shoulder the port goes in?" I asked.

"No," the doctor replied.

"Put it in my left shoulder," I said. "Turkey season starts in April, and I don't want it to interfere with shooting a shotgun."

Incredulous, the ladies slowly swiveled their heads and leveled withering gazes upon me.

"You've got cancer, and you're worried about turkey hunting?" asked Laura coolly.

"I'll be alive in April," I said with a shrug. "I'm not going to miss turkey season."

My doctor stared intensely. After a long silence, he said resolutely, "I think YOU are going to be okay."

As the outdoors editor for a large daily newspaper in Arkansas, I live what many consider a dream. I hunt and fish several times a week and, thanks to the wonders of digital technology, I chronicle my adventures for a worldwide audience in print, photography, and video. I won't try to convince you otherwise: It is the best job in journalism.

Readers often ask what I enjoy most.

"Whatever I'm doing at the time," I answer.

That is true, but if given an ultimatum, I would choose hunting wild turkeys in the spring. I would, however, request a longer season and a more generous limit. I love the challenge and the intimate interaction of bantering with a wild gobbler. I'm one-on-one with one of the wariest animals in the forest. It's my wits and instincts against his keen senses. So many things can and do go wrong, and so few things go right.

Unlike deer hunting, where remote cameras enable us to pattern and pursue individual bucks, a turkey hunter must tilt with any bird that answers his challenge. You may know a four-year-old gobbler with a horsetail beard is in your woods, but if an irrepressible two-year-old gobbler answers your call, he will probably be your lone partner for that particular dance. Some of us will pass on that two-year-old bird for an opportunity to woo an older bird, not only for his longer beard and spurs but also because he's usually a harder bird to kill.

Every turkey hunt is different. Whatever happened in the last hunt seldom applies to the next hunt, but every nuance of every hunt is a thread in the tapestry of experience that makes a turkey hunter more competent and ultimately more successful. I share my stories not so much about the kills, but about the birds, the chases, and the exhilarating moments of our encounters. Applying a tag to a gobbler is incidental to everything else that encompasses a hunt. Turkey hunting is like a video game that you never beat. You merely advance to the next level.

The memories are equally about the people who shared in and contributed to the adventures. I have met some of my dearest friends through a shared joy of hunting, often because of something I wrote that resonated with them. We share our most immense joys, and we shoulder one another's burdens during our most desolate trials.

Each bird is a gift. It's a cause for celebration and a symbol of my gratitude to life, living, and the Giver of life. A mature wild gobbler is a work of art, and like all great art, the beauty is in the story behind it.

This collection is a tribute to the Kings of Spring and to the friends who picked me up off the mat in times of failure, sponged the blood from my cuts, and nudged me back into the ring. In my darkest hours, they inspired me to fight to live another day.

CHAPTER ONE

BAPTISM

I heard Todd Craighead's voice before I saw his face.
Craighead didn't speak. He yelped like a hen turkey. His office mate, Josh Cussimanio, replied with a throaty gobble. Two other gobbles erupted from different offices down the hall. Not a word was spoken.

The date was March 1, 1998, and it was my first day as the new information specialist for the Oklahoma Department of Wildlife Conservation (ODWC). Craighead, who battles arthrogryposis, a rare and debilitating congenital disorder that disables joints and connective tissue, is the longtime host of the popular *Outdoor Oklahoma* television program. Cussimanio, a taciturn Kansan, is a wildlife biologist who served as the agency's aquatic education coordinator. Their bird banter was the opening dialogue in my turkey hunting saga.

On March 1, 1998, I knew nothing about turkeys or turkey hunting. Eastern, Rio Grande, Merriam's, Osceola, and Gould's were fraternal vernacular to me, but I corked my ignorance and absorbed information from experienced hunters who, in their excitement over the upcoming spring turkey season, flung open their knowledge vaults. Those sessions often occurred in staff meetings that began with our supervisor Rich Fuller quizzing us about our latest hunting exploits. Turkey hunters are inveterate storytellers. Once they start talking, they are easily coaxed into revealing their most closely held secrets.

My job as the agency's spokesman also gave me unlimited access to some of the nation's top turkey biologists. While not a turkey hunter at that time, I was an experienced journalist with a highly refined knack for interrogative conversation. I quickly assimilated a working knowledge of wild turkeys, wild turkey conservation, and wild turkey management without a shred of experience actually hunting them.

The hunting community is composed of specialists that exhibit distinctive traits. Deer hunters are technical and detail oriented. They obsess over barometric pressures, wind direction, seasonal food sources, and antler characteristics of individual animals.

In his book, *U2 at the End of the World*, Bill Flanagan cited an incident that occurred when U2 band members Bono and Adam Clayton hitchhiked in Tennessee. A teenager blasting Def Leppard's "Pour Some Sugar on Me" in his stereo gave the musicians a ride. Recognizing his passengers, the driver quickly swapped out a U2 CD, but Bono perceived a revelation. Kids don't buy audio equipment to play their music. They buy music to play their audio equipment. *Achtung Baby* was U2's sonic recalibration to that reality.

Waterfowl hunters are in that group. They don't buy gear for hunting. They hunt to use their gear. Their retrieving dogs are their proxies. An inept or poorly behaved retriever reflects badly on its owner. A hunter with an exceptional retriever is a preferred citizen with a standing invitation to hunt in company above his social or economic status.

To an even greater extent, upland bird hunters live vicariously through their bird dogs. For them, the hunt is all about steady points and difficult retrieves. Bird hunters are very proud of their shotguns, but they almost never mention shooting. Unless another hunter compliments a companion's exceptional shot, such talk is considered vulgar.

Turkey hunters are driven by mysterious forces from an uncharted universe. Their antennae are tuned to frequencies carrying voices that frighten even the most committed pursuers of other game. Avid deer and duck hunters often decline my turkey hunting invitations. They lust for the high, but the threat of addiction terrifies them.

A turkey hunter's desire to work gobblers is a consumptive addiction for which he will sacrifice his money, time, relationships, and even his health. Jackie Rauls and Wayne Richardson, longtime friends from south Arkansas, spent nearly a decade hunting as many states as time allowed in a season. They started annually in Florida and worked west, taking Osceola, Eastern, Rio Grande, and Merriam's gobblers to log multiple Grand Slams, the feat of tagging one of each of the four North American subspecies in one season. The friendships they established during their odyssey provided them additional places to hunt and stretched their springs to the cusps of summer.

Regardless of location, Rauls and Richardson always suspended hunting on Sundays to attend church. Rauls recalled asking a pastor in Iowa if they were welcome to worship with his flock.

"Of course you are," the pastor replied, "but you should be aware of some unique divisions within our congregation."

"Oh?" Rauls asked, suspicious. Preachers are notoriously reluctant to acknowledge divisions in their flocks, especially to strangers.

"Yes," the pastor continued. "Republicans sit on the right side of the aisle. Democrats sit on the left side."

"I think we can handle that," Rauls said, amused.

"Oh, but there's more," the pastor continued. "The Chevrolet people sit in these rows here. The Ford people sit in those pews, and the Dodge people sit in those pews."

"Where do the Toyota people sit?" Rauls asked, mischievously.

The pastor stared at Rauls blankly and replied indifferently, "If one shows up, I reckon we can find a place for him."

"That won't be necessary," Rauls said, laughing. "We'll fit in just fine without all that."

Adorning the front of Craighead's cubicle is the cape and fan of his first Eastern gobbler, which he killed in Kansas while hunting with Cussimanio. Although the Rio Grande is the prevalent wild turkey subspecies in the Sooner State, Oklahomans revere the Eastern subspecies because of its reputation for being so difficult to hunt and because opportunities to hunt Eastern turkeys in Oklahoma are so limited. They inhabit a narrow slice of eastern Oklahoma and are managed under special regulations in a southeastern portion of the state. Hunting Eastern birds at Honobia Creek Wildlife Management Area (WMA), Three Rivers WMA, or Pushmataha WMA is a pilgrimage. Only after I left Oklahoma for permanent relocation into Eastern wild turkey territory did I finally understand the obsession.

Another member of the ODWC's turkey hunting fraternity was Brian Barger, an Oklahoma State University graduate in wildlife biology who was serving as an intern with the ODWC's Project WILD education program. Barger's baritone nasal drawl and easygoing manner belied fierce competitiveness that revealed itself daily in our lunchtime horseshoe tournaments behind the agency's motor pool.

I stole Barger from another employee in our education section to which he was assigned, but his supervisor agreed that Barger's creative talents were better suited to the agency's public affairs component. Under this aegis, Barger and I traveled around the state chronicling the ODWC's mission. Barger shot video, and I wrote news releases and magazine articles. One of our first projects together was documenting a special turkey hunt in the McCurtain County Wilderness Area in southeastern Oklahoma that was held for the first time in 1999. The wilderness area was closed to hunting at that time, but the wildlife department made an exception for a special auction hunt that was personally guided by ODWC Director Greg Duffy. Part of the package was for the constituent to star in a commemorative video memorializing the hunt. For three days Barger and I idled around Broken Bow Lake in a rented party barge, waiting for a summons to recreate the hunt and capture its joyous aftermath. We spent that time fishing, which made us feel self-conscious. You're not supposed to have that much fun on the clock, especially on the public's dime.

Late in the last day, we grew anxious wondering if we had missed the call, so we sped to the rendezvous point. Eventually Duffy and his hunter arrived empty-handed and surly. The hunter had blown two chances at gobblers that Duffy had called close, and Duffy chastened him with a few playful but pointed barbs.

As very junior employees, Barger and I ignored their repartee. Duffy was our boss, but the hunter was a wealthy constituent that had paid a lot of money for a once-only opportunity. Inadvertently insulting a person like that by sharing in the mirth could have repercussions on one's career that he might never realize. Barger distanced himself from the tension by taking light meter readings for his video camera while I jotted a few items in my notepad.

My last big project with Barger was creating a promotional package for the official dedication of Hackberry Flat Wildlife

Management Area, a state-of-the-art wetland reclamation project near Frederick, Oklahoma. The ODWC later named a wildlife observation tower at Hackberry Flat in Barger's honor.

With no full-time employment opportunities available for the foreseeable future in the ODWC's video department, I convinced Barger that his future was in writing. I taught him the craft of writing news releases and coached him through the articles he wrote for *Outdoor Oklahoma* magazine. When articulating a wildlife agency's message, a spokesperson must carefully choose every word and construct every sentence so that the meaning is clear, with no room for adverse interpretation. Furthermore, the writer must also respect the sensitivities of the hunters, anglers, and trappers that finance the agency through their purchases of hunting, fishing, and trapping licenses.

For example, the perpetually cash-strapped agency lobbied the Oklahoma legislature to enact a statewide conservation sales tax to provide additional funding to hunting and fishing license sales. While conservation groups such as Ducks Unlimited and the National Wild Turkey Federation understood that the agency worked miracles with loaves and fishes, convincing the public to pay more was a hard sell.

"Why should they?" I asked Barger. "Oklahoma has some of the best deer and turkey hunting in the country. We are America's quail hunting capital. We've got great duck and goose hunting. Our pheasant hunting is ascendent. We've got sandhill cranes. We have great elk hunting and even hunting for pronghorn antelope. We have great fishing for bass, stripers, paddlefish, and even trout. Our wildlife management areas are showcases. We're doing all of this with current funding, so convince me—a guy with greasy, skinned-up knuckles turning wrenches in a sweltering garage all day—that

I need to pay more to hunt a few precious hours on weekends. A lot of our constituents make minimum wage, and they depend on game and fish to eat. Respect that guy in everything you write and say. Convince him what a little more will do for him. He doesn't give a rat's ass what a little more will do for us."

It is a delicate balance, and Barger deftly mastered the genre because he was a country boy of modest means who never forgot his roots. He wrote as if he were chatting with his neighbors back home in northeastern Oklahoma.

In exchange, Barger tutored me in his immense knowledge of turkey hunting. He was an expert at mimicking turkey vocalizations with his own voice, a skill that I never acquired. Remarkably, we never hunted together. His uncharacteristic elusiveness for a few weeks in the springtime was my first exposure to a turkey hunter's propensity to shun companionship during turkey season. His turkey tutorials occurred while driving or chatting in my office.

I considered Barger a kid brother, and I was very proud when he was hired into my position after I left the department in 2000.

My initial interest in turkey hunting was mercenary. I wanted to fit in with this bunch. I admired my peers. I craved their approval, but more importantly, I believed that my lack of experience was a credibility barrier with my colleagues and with the agency's constituents. That changed shortly after I started work but not because of wild turkeys. I took my wife and my three young sons camping in the Ouachita National Forest in western Arkansas. After supper, I walked my four-year-old son Daniel to our tent for bed. A timber rattlesnake bit me on the bare top of a sandaled foot and hospitalized me for a weekend.

"Isn't that just precious!" I groused. "I'm on initial probation, missing work for a nonwork-related injury in a different state. They'll fire my ass for sure."

Just the opposite happened. Word got around the department quickly, and employees came from all over the state to meet the new snakebit guy. My acceptance into the conservation club was immediate and unconditional.

Cussimanio's unsolicited interest in teaching me how to hunt turkeys was also mercenary. He had permission to hunt a large farm in Canadian County near El Reno. The farm was rich with game and even had a duck marsh adjacent to the South Canadian River. Cussimanio wanted to lease the farm, but he needed partners to defray the cost. On April 20, 1999, he invited me on a recruiting visit disguised as a turkey hunt.

The morning started with blueprint precision. A flock of Rio Grande turkeys roosting in a line of cottonwood trees fluttered into the corner of an alfalfa field about seventy-five yards in front of us. The air trembled in the heat, creating a rippling effect over the vast sea of young alfalfa sprouts undulating in the breeze. The hens descended first, followed by three mature gobblers. It was the first time I had seen turkeys fly off a roost, and the sight of such big birds barreling clumsily to the ground was comical.

They started straight for us but then veered into a brushy wood-lot to our right. With his latex mouth call, Cussimanio pleaded with the turkeys to reveal themselves, but they stayed in cover and tormented us with flickering glimpses as they paraded back and forth through the thicket. Finally, I lay prone and peered under the brush, but I saw only legs and thighs. Eventually, the turkeys about-faced, filtered out the back of the thicket and marched into a deep crease at the far end of the field.

"We probably should have belly crawled closer," Cussimanio said. "We might have been able to shoot a bird or two, but I didn't know if you'd be comfortable with that."

It didn't matter. Those birds plunged their spurs deep into my imagination. I had never experienced anything so thrilling, and from that moment, turkey hunting was my personal mission.

After leaving the farm, I visited the University of Oklahoma library to pick up a folder of photographs. I drove a bare-bones, base model 1990 Nissan pickup truck that had no accessories, not even an AM radio. Unaware of the day's news, I entered the library dressed in camouflage. The place went deathly silent, and students froze as their eyes locked upon me. A few discreetly vanished among the bookshelves. Finally, a young, bespectacled librarian with a receding hairline approached timidly and asked in a quavering stutter if he could assist me.

"Yes, I'm Bryan Hendricks with the Wildlife Department," I replied airily. "I'm here to pick up some photographs for *Outdoor Oklahoma* magazine."

"Oh, thank God!" the librarian whispered with a loud sigh. "Yes, YES! I have them. Come with me!"

Everybody seemed to exhale at once, but their eyes remained fixed on me until the door closed behind me. That reception mystified me until I returned to my office and heard about the massacre at Columbine High School in Colorado. The shooting was in progress when I entered the library, and those OU students surely thought I was a copycat terrorist. In the context of the moment, that meek librarian exhibited uncommon bravery to approach me alone. Horrified, I called him and apologized. Ever after, I change into street clothes before I engage with the public after a hunt.

While I joined Cussimanio and several other coworkers in leasing that farm, we didn't hunt together again. Hunting solo, I committed the most egregious rookie errors. Instead of setting up near gobblers at dawn, I perched against roost trees and called to birds gobbling right over my head as they heaved to and fro on their perches. I tailed gobblers through the woods instead of maneuvering around them or sitting tight to call in solitary toms.

Though futile, those exercises weren't fruitless. For example, one gobbler that left a roost over my head went straight to an open area that I call a strutting green. It's a subtle opening in the woods where gobblers go to display. Gobblers can be seen from a distance there, and the strutting greens are natural places for them to collect hens.

From there, that gobbler went straight to the deep crease in the field where the turkeys retreated during my hunt with Cussimanio. A copse of shrubs and small trees in the crease provided cover for the tom, and he gobbled from that spot for about twenty minutes. The acoustics of the bowl amplified and resonated his gobbles, projecting them farther than if the bird had gobbled from an open field or from the woods. That taught me to look for these little gobbling auditoriums because a gobbler is like any other rock star. He loves the sound of his own voice.

In August 2000, I took a job with the Missouri Department of Conservation and moved to the Miller County hamlet of Mary's Home. I had yet to kill a spring gobbler, but that was at the height of Missouri's turkey hunting boom. When a neighbor invited me to hunt a prime property near the Osage River, I had every reason to believe I would finally earn my mythical turkey hunting merit badge.

Missouri's spring turkey season always opens on a Monday. One week before the 2001 opener, the landowner showed me a narrow creek bottom where turkeys roosted. At dusk, from the shadows of a forested ridge amid the squeaky din of mating spring peepers, we watched a squadron of turkeys fly up to roost in the trees over the creek. The big birds are almost as awkward flying onto a roost as they are flying down.

On the Saturday before the opener, I visited the farm for a last round of reconnaissance. I arrived after dawn and crept amid the tall trees on the side of the ridge overlooking the pasture. About fifteen turkeys were in the field, including a half dozen gobblers. There was no doubt which gobbler was dominant. Lacking only a robe and scepter, he strutted the entire length of the field. The other toms half-displayed deferentially. I left them to scout the other side of the farm where I heard additional turkeys in the dense cover of a ravine.

Confident that I would have two options on Monday, I returned to the field to check on the morning flock before leaving the farm for the weekend. Seeing the field empty, I made yet another rookie error. Unaware that the turkeys were loafing out of sight at the foot of the ridge, I pressed aggressively on a push-button yelper. Two toms gobbled from below. I shouldn't have called, but when those birds answered, I should have run back to the truck. Instead, I did precisely the wrong thing. I called again. The gobblers responded, this time much closer. They were coming fast.

Compounding my predicament was my attire. Instead of camouflage, I wore blue jeans and a black T-shirt, with no gloves or face covering. It was too late to flee, so I crouched against a cedar tree, turned my face downward and froze. Peeking under the bill of my ball cap, I glimpsed a rapturous vision. At the crest of the ridge a mere fifteen yards away, among a small grove of white-laced dogwoods and velvety redbuds, two gobblers bellowed for supremacy. With necks stretched forward and tails stretched back, they flung their heads forward and roared.

To my great relief, they did not appear to notice me, nor did they linger. They gobbled all the way back down the ridge and back into the field. That incident taught me a valuable lesson. Don't call when scouting. Recon is a silent, stealthy business.

In the darkness of opening morning, I crept down the ridge and erected a small fabric screen in a semicircle beside a cedar hedge that separated two fields. A narrow gap formed a pinch point through which turkeys would funnel, provided they still roosted in the same spot. I placed a hen decoy about thirty yards away and planted my seat behind the screen with my back against a wall of cedars.

Wood thrushes greeted the brightening sky as mosquitoes whined in my ears. I pumped insect repellent in my cupped right hand and rubbed it on my neck, ears, and face. My hands itched from contact with the cedars, and the friction from my gloves made them burn.

Soon, whip-poor-wills chimed in with the thrushes and cardinals, accompanied by occasional rejoinders from barred owls. The curtain had risen, prompting the gobblers to chuckle from the far end of the field. I congratulated myself. This was going to be a quick hit. I visualized marching out of that field with the boss gobbler slung over my shoulder, emailing all my friends and humbly accepting their hearty congratulations. I might even get to work on time, and of course I would spend the entire morning reliving the triumph with my colleagues.

Minutes later, I saw the turkeys. Like two days before, the boss gobbler strutted and swayed. The subordinate gobblers displayed in half measure, walking ahead of the boss like footmen. All the turkeys passed through the gap in the hedge except for the boss gobbler, which peeled away and pranced straight to my decoy. Puffed up like a Prussian general, he strutted all around it. Then, he positioned to mount the decoy. I made a single cluck with my mouth call. The gobbler deflated his plumage and stood erect, exposing his neck.

In the intensity of the moment, I did not hear the shot, but my head and shoulder reeled from the recoil of my Winchester pump loaded with Winchester Supreme three-inch turkey loads. The gobbler collapsed but quickly righted and dashed like the Road Runner cartoon character toward the hill on the opposite side of the field. I fired again, but it was too late. I spent the next forty minutes combing the hillside desperately hoping to find the gobbler, but I knew it was pointless. In sports parlance, I choked. This game was over.

Like reliving a car accident, I replayed the scene in my mind for days. I made two critical errors. One, the decoy was too far from my blind. Fifteen yards would have been about right, especially since I was virtually invisible against the cedars. Even if the gobbler detected me before reaching the decoy, he still would have been well within killing range.

Unquestionably, the definitive error was failing to pattern my shotgun. Experienced turkey hunters assured me that my extra-full-constriction turkey choke would throw a tea-saucer-size pattern to at least thirty yards. Therefore, I assumed it would throw a lethal pattern to at least forty yards. Without actually patterning the gun, any assumption was baseless. Patterning a shotgun is Hunting 101. Neglecting that detail cost me a gobbler.

I often make fun of my late father for doing the same thing with his deer rifle. Dad was a brilliant attorney, but he was capable of some astonishing misconceptions, like the time he marveled at a meteor streaking through the sky while we drove to a duck hunt in southeast Arkansas.

"I wonder how many years ago that thing fell?" Dad mused.

"What do you mean, how many years ago did it fall?" I asked.

"It takes millions of years for the light from a star to reach earth," he said. "I wonder how many light-years ago that star fell."

"That was a piece of space debris burning up in the atmosphere," I said hesitantly, unsure if he was joking. "It happened just now, about fifty miles above us up in the thermosphere. Stars don't fall. They just burn out."

"Bullshit!" Dad retorted, and the fight was on.

For years, Dad hunted deer with a Remington 742 semi-automatic rifle with factory iron sights. He was so proud when he finally mounted a scope, but he refused to sight it in—to calibrate point of aim with point of impact.

"Don't need to sight it in," he huffed. "It's got a scope."

Dad reasoned that the scope's mere presence made the rifle accurate, process be damned. Then came the day when he fired an entire magazine of ammo at a deer without effect. He insisted that the rifle was at fault. Therefore, sighting in the scope could not correct a defective rifle. Instead, he quit hunting deer because he didn't trust his rifle. One hour at a range and half a box of ammunition would have settled that question for a lifetime.

For better or worse, I am my father's son, but I learned my lesson. I pattern whenever I use a new turkey load, choke tube, or shotgun. It matters a lot. I have seen premium turkey ammo that wouldn't pattern through top-grade barrels and custom chokes, and I have seen ordinary shotguns throw wickedly dense patterns with ordinary pheasant loads. Practice begets knowledge, and knowledge is power.

In early 2001, I moved to California, Missouri, a small town about twenty-five miles west of Jefferson City. My daily drive to the office on US Highway 50 took me past a farm where I often saw turkeys. On Nov. 8, 2001, a lone gobbler stood in full display on a high spot in the middle of a field. A wooded hillside ringed the field like a ragged lace hem. The golden leaves of the black walnut trees in October were now the color of manila paper, and the reds of the maples looked like dried blood. The gobbler faced the highway and seemed to watch me as I sped past. The wind rippled through his fan and tousled his plumage. His head glowed unusually deep shades of scarlet and blue in the autumn light.

"How odd for a turkey to display like that in the fall," I mused. "Man, I wish Barger were here to see this!"

When I got to my office, I turned on my computer and checked my emails. I had a new message from Cussimanio, who moved to the Missouri Department of Conservation a few months before I did. The subject line prompted me to call him immediately. My grip weakened on the receiver and my throat tightened when Cussimanio told me the news. Barger died in his sleep early that morning, apparently from an undiagnosed congenital cardiac condition. He was 29 years old.

I think about that November gobbler often. I believe it is possible for the spirits of our loved ones to reach out to us when they cross to the other side, or maybe the Good Lord does it on their behalf in forms that are indelible. Either way, I believe that gobbler was Brian Barger saying goodbye.

CHAPTER TWO

OZZY

During my years in Missouri, my constant companion was a neighbor known to his friends as Meadowlark Clark, an accomplished Kansas City chef who, with his wife, Patricia, opened a catering service in the town of California, the Moniteau County seat about twenty-five miles west of Jefferson City.

California, a traditional high school football powerhouse, is a picturesque Midwestern village amid the rolling hills of the Osage Plains. Its centerpiece is a Classic Revival courthouse that towers over the highest point in the town square, which also included a Latino grocery store, a tavern, a law office, and the Fraternal Order of the Eagles Aerie #4027. On hot summer nights, the aerie doors were often left open, oozing a cloud of cigarette smoke that hovered over the sidewalk like a fog over a fen. The interior looked like a saloon from a Sergio Leone western with an oily patina of tobacco tar covering every surface. Even a brief visit left one's throat dry and scratchy.

One of our neighbors was an amiable fellow of simple needs and simple means named Floyd. Then in his forties, he lived with his elderly mother who forbade him from entering her house. He slept in a plywood hut next to the garage. Its interior was illuminated by a garage work light that dangled through a hole in the ceiling on an extension cord. Floyd drove a creaky, clattering Ranchero, an ungainly pickup truck/sedan hybrid that was Ford's counterpoint to Chevrolet's El Camino. During his infrequent sessions behind its wheel, Floyd was the picture of bliss. Because the vehicle was usually disabled, Floyd usually walked, but he was often resourceful in finding alternative means of transportation.

For example, one evening I looked toward the square and saw Floyd weaving down the hill on a riding lawnmower. Slung across the cowling in plastic bags were two cases of beer. He was less than a block from home when he swerved into a concrete drainage ditch. The wreck destroyed the mower and most of its cargo, but Floyd was miraculously unhurt.

Next door lived a large family from Zacatecas, Mexico. The adults worked in a local poultry processing mill. Their youngest son, who was about five years old, gave himself an impromptu circumcision when, trying to scandalize my children, he snagged his penis in the web-wire fence between our homes. Panicked, he ripped free and left his foreskin hanging in the fence.

Cherry Mash, a unique candy bar made in St. Joseph, is ubiquitous throughout Missouri. Produced continuously since 1918, it features a soft, cherry-flavored center containing maraschino cherries inside a shell of chocolate and peanuts. Every store sells it, but nobody admits to actually eating one. One night at the California IGA, I approached two female employees who were restocking a shelf. One was a teenager. The other was in her late fifties.

"Are these Cherry Mash things any good?" I asked, brandishing the distinctive white and red package.

"Yuck! They're nasty!" declared the teenager.

"You hush!" retorted the elder. "That's good candy!"

"It is not," replied the younger. "It sucks!"

"You be quiet!" the elder snarled. "I've eaten them all my life." She turned to me and said sweetly, "It's one of my favorites. You'll love it."

The elder seemed not so much enamored with Cherry Mash as she was honor bound to defend from this impertinent youth the virtue of a venerable Missouri product. They argued so bitterly that they forgot about me. The elder looked positively radiant when I finally interrupted them by announcing, "You sold me. I'm gonna try it." She flashed a triumphant smirk at her adversary before leading me to the register.

"We won't give you a refund!" the teenager shouted scornfully at our backs.

Scenes like these compose the tableau of daily life in the heart of midwestern turkey country, and in its midst lived a serene, yogi-like figure that became one of my closest friends. I met Meadowlark Clark when I answered an ad about German shorthaired pointer puppies for sale on an index card tacked to a bulletin board at one of California's two convenience stores. Beside it was another index card that said, "$50 says I can outfish you at your best hole. Call (573) . . . "

This tackboard troll aroused my curiosity. I called the number. Its owner said he had never won that bet, but for fifty dollars he got to fish the best private lakes and ponds in mid-Missouri.

"That's a whole lot cheaper than a guided fishing trip on Lake of the Ozarks or Truman [Reservoir]," he said, "and the fishing is way better."

Meadowlark and I were both avid upland bird hunters, and the puppy purchase was the portal to a friendship that soon saw us chasing quail, doves, and woodcocks across central and northern

Missouri. We hunted a different public conservation area every weekend, and our travels familiarized me with the state whose tax-payers and sportsmen I served.

My daughters named the pup Sally. She was a sweetheart, but her parents' hunting genes did not trickle to her low place in the lit-ter. Good bird dogs live for bird scent and for the rush of the flush, and they are driven to find it. Those traits eluded Sally, who was content to walk behind me. Once, while hunting quail at Overton Bottoms Wildlife Management Area near Rocheport, she balked at going through a brushy covert. I shouldered through the tangle, and Sally followed so closely that the upsweep of my heel repeatedly smacked her chin.

I never had a good bird dog, so I got proficient in my youth at hunting without dogs. I learned to recognize bobwhite hiding places such as plum thickets, brushy tangles, brambles, or weedy patches at the edges of fields or cutovers, or even under low cedar branches. Maybe Sally just needed inspiration. If I showed her a covey, perhaps its scent would unsheathe her pointing instinct. If she saw a bird fall, she would piece together the rest. I eased toward a cluster of young persimmon trees. Sally did not get "birdy," but I certainly did. I felt the tension of nearby bobwhites poised to flush.

"Sally, up here, baby!" I said with quiet urgency.

Sally looked at me quizzically and wagged her stub nervously as she tried to process the brusqueness of my tone. She refused to advance.

Okay, I thought. *Maybe if I flush the birds...*

I took three tentative steps forward and kicked a branch in a weed patch, provoking eight or nine bobwhites to burst almost from beneath my soles. Sally's approving expression was like that of a child watching a magician at a birthday party. I thrust my shotgun toward her and said, "Here, dog, I'll point, and you shoot!"

This greatly amused Meadowlark, who was something of a hunting-dog whisperer. Our last quail hunt together was at Union Ridge Conservation Area in extreme northern Missouri near the Iowa border. Driving north in a heavy snowstorm was like being in a Grand Theft Auto video game as cars and trucks twirled off the highway and into the ditches ahead of us and even beside us. With Meadowlark's Ford F-150 King Ranch Edition in four-wheel drive, we barreled through the melee like a tank.

We tromped through deep snow all day without success. Driving back, headlamp beams ricocheted through a blizzard, creating a blinding glare over a sea of black ice. Meadowlark lowered the windows and inhaled an endless chain of cigarettes. He leaned forward in a near meditational state, knuckles white against the wheel in the glow of the dashboard lights.

"You okay?" I asked, shivering from the intense cold.

"Man, I am freaking stressed out!" Meadowlark croaked, the cherry of his burning cigarette glowing from the left corner of his pinched lips.

"Why don't you take a break and let me drive awhile?" I offered.

"I'm good," Meadowlark muttered determinedly, unwilling to trust his beloved Ford to another man.

Quail season's autumn yielded to winter and duck hunting, another of our mutual passions. Meadowlark and I pursued ducks at conservation areas along the Missouri River where we perfected a technique of jump-shooting mallards on remote ponds. One such hunt took place on an icy day at Marion Bottoms Conservation Area, when I foolishly boasted that my shotgun virtually eliminated the rude recoil of 3 ½-inch, 12-gauge shotgun shells.

"When I shoot at game, I don't notice it at all," I said.

Meadowlark expressed skepticism with one slow, half-twist of his head.

The gun was the Winchester Super X2 that had helped transform my turkey hunting fortunes. I did not use 3 ½-inch shells for
turkeys, but for ducks I believed that they gave me the extra range
to take down the "tall ones." I used a screw-in Poly-Choke on the
X-Full setting with No. 2 steel shot. Though it clashed garishly with
the gun's graceful lines, the bulbous choke squeezed the massive shot
charge into a ridiculously tight pattern that killed ducks so high and
with such authority that a game warden once checked my ammo,
believing I was shooting lead pellets, which is illegal for waterfowl.

Meadowlark and I stood on a high bluff about sixty feet above
the Missouri River near the Hartsburg Access. Before us was a long
slough that met the river by way of a narrow, shallow ditch that
was imperceptible from the river behind a logjam piled about eight
feet high. When the river floods, it backs into the slough and then
fills the woods in the conservation area. During a flood, the river
also recharges a series of small ponds and lakes that the river gouged
during previous floods. Hidden by vast, dense thickets, these remote
"blew" holes offer superb duck hunting when open water is present.

Hearing a barrage of gunfire to the north, we plowed through
the woods until we encountered the logjam separating the slough
from the river. We climbed the ridge and saw duck hunters on the
opposite bank. Using driftwood, they had assembled a makeshift
blind that overlooked a large stretch of open water behind three
sandbars and a wing dam. Over the next hour, dozens of ducks
poured into that hole. Some of those ducks banked over us, passing
almost head high above the ridgetop.

A mallard drake streaked over, and I fired straight up while
twisting my back and hips in the follow-through. Standing on ice,
I lost my balance under the recoil and fell on my back, sliding backward into an icy bowl before slamming into a fallen log. The drake
hit the ice with a thud and came to rest beside me.

Struggling to my feet, I hoisted the drake triumphantly. Pooching his lips skyward, Meadowlark blew a cloud of cigarette smoke, turned, and averted his face toward the river. That was the last time I fired a 3 ½-inch shotgun shell. Many hunters use them for turkeys, but the logic behind needing or even desiring that degree of firepower to kill a twenty-pound bird mystifies me. I cannot explain why I ever felt them necessary to kill four-pound ducks.

When warm weather finally arrived, Meadowlark and I discovered that we also shared a love for fishing. Days on the water first acquainted me with Meadowlark's casual disregard for detail, and him with my near fanatical devotion to the same. Our first clash occurred when we drove halfway across the state to fish for white bass at Truman Reservoir. Meadowlark crowed about all the great food he brought for the gourmet shore lunch he had planned.

Anticipating this feast sustained us through a taxing morning of rough water and poor fishing. Famished, we beached the boat on a sandy bank at lunchtime. Meadowlark opened his cooler, but it contained only a couple of Johnsonville bratwursts infused with some kind of cheese product. He also forgot the charcoal, so we roasted the brats over a meager driftwood fire that made the brats taste like soap.

That miscue presaged our ill-fated canoe trip on Moniteau Creek. We carried the canoe in my truck to our launch site at a public access. Meadowlark arranged for his truck to be parked at another public access about seven river miles downstream. When we reached the boat ramp after an exhausting day of portaging over snake-infested logjams, Meadowlark's truck was absent. It was also absent at the next ramp downstream. With the sun setting, I contemplated the perilous prospect of paddling all the way to the Missouri River in the dark. Thankfully, Meadowlark's truck awaited us at the last access in the chain.

Roiling Meadowlark's characteristic calmness was the untimely expiration of his cigarette lighter shortly after we launched. Its failure condemned him to a hot, humid day in the throes of morbid nicotine withdrawals.

While casual about most hunting, Meadowlark was deadly serious about turkeys. He taught me a lot over the next few years, especially about turkey behavior in the middle of the day. Particularly valuable were his observations about turkeys gravitating to fields in the late morning and early afternoon.

Our first spring hunt together was at Lamine River Conservation Area near Tipton, Missouri, a small town known among classic rock lovers as the birthplace and burial place of Gene Clark, a founding member of The Byrds. Gene Clark was a vastly underrated performer and songwriter, and his departure from the Byrds was the tug of the thread that ultimately unraveled the band's fabric. His solo album, *No Other*, is a masterpiece. It is also his epitaph.

Named for a Missouri River tributary, Lamine River Conservation Area contains a patchwork of agricultural fields and thin woodlots among gently rolling hills separated by steep, shallow ravines. While hunting woodcocks the previous fall, Meadowlark and I found a chunk of promising turkey habitat in a remote corner where other hunters were unlikely to venture. As we drove through the darkness for our first turkey hunt together, we eagerly discussed the latest tips that Meadowlark had gleaned from his hunting magazines.

"Did you read that article in the latest *Turkey & Turkey Hunting* about mid-morning calling techniques?" Meadowlark asked.

"That one in the rack next to your commode?" I asked.

"Yeah," Meadowlark replied.

"I tried to, but the pages were all stuck together," I said. "Man, you must really get off on gobbler porn!"

"Ha, ha. Very funny," Meadowlark sighed with a long-suffering grimace.

Meadowlark and I sat side by side at the edge of a field with a thicket at our backs and waited for a gobbler to bid us good morning. To our surprise, a hen yelped softly from a tree about thirty yards behind us. Before long, a gobbler sounded from the far side of the field. The hen got louder, and soon a change in the timbre of the gobbles indicated that the tom was on the ground and approaching.

A gently rising slope crested about fifty yards away, limiting our vision to that distance. Meadowlark and I fretted that the hen would spoil the hunt. With the gobbles getting louder, the hen pitched down about twenty yards in front of us. She fluffed her feathers with a rolling, side-to-side shake and started walking toward the gobbler. If they met, she would lead him away from us.

"She's going to ruin everything!" I hissed. "We've got to get her out of here!"

Meadowlark stood and waved his arms. The hen looked at him quizzically, as turkeys often do when processing an abrupt stimulus. Meadowlark then charged the hen. She flew back into the woods behind us, perched in a tree and putt-putted.

Meadowlark heaved his chest indignantly toward the hen and mouthed an expletive. We chuckled quietly as he returned to our lair. Meanwhile, the gobbler kept coming. With our guns resting on our arched knees, we ignored our burning muscles and tried to calm our pounding hearts.

"How are we going to do this?" Meadowlark whispered.

"If he comes to the left, I'll take him," I said. "If he's to the right, he's yours."

"What if he comes straight down the middle?" Meadowlark asked.

"On the count of three, we both shoot him." I said.

Meadowlark nodded, knowing full well that we'd both shoot on "two."

Anticipation throbbed like an E-string on a bass guitar. With my nerves on a razor's edge, a screeching voice jolted me as if I had grabbed an electrified wire.

"All ABOARRRRD! Ahh, hah, hah hah!"

The intro to Ozzy Osbourne's "Crazy Train," howled from a cell phone embedded in the pocket of a T-shirt beneath a pullover inside Meadowlark's bib overalls. The tom belted out a mighty shock gobble. As Ozzy shrieked, Meadowlark frantically clawed for the phone buried deep within his armor.

"You might as well answer the goddamn thing," I said glumly as Meadowlark ripped a glove from his free hand and tried to silence the device.

"Hello? Hi, Honey. Well, no, it's really not a good time. We're working a gobbler," Meadowlark murmured into his phone.

"'Not anymore," I muttered.

"What's that?" Meadowlark asked, pushing his face toward me while shielding the phone with his hand.

"Good morning, Patty!" I said cheerily.

"Bryan says hi," Meadowlark relayed. "Hey, I'll be home in a couple of hours. Love you too. Bye, Honey."

Meadowlark and I sat silently as I contemplated the most absurd implosion of a hunt to date. A few minutes later, a shot boomed from a far edge across the field.

"Somebody just killed our bird," I said. "Thanks for nothing, Ozzy, you no-turkey-killing mother f . . . "

"Sorry about that," Meadowlark interrupted meekly. "I thought I turned the ringer off."

"Seriously? You brought a phone to the turkey woods?" I asked mockingly. "Next time, leave it in the truck. Better yet, leave it at home!"

"So, that means there'll be a next time?" Meadowlark asked hopefully.

We stared straight ahead, tension crackling. From another pocket Meadowlark exhumed a pack of Pall Malls, tapped a cigarette free from the cluster, pulled it from the opening with his lips, and lit it with a flick of his disposable lighter. He inhaled deeply, tilted back his head, and savored the draw. When he exhaled, his body trembled as he let out a deep, raspy laugh.

"It's not funny, Clark," I growled. He laughed even harder, causing him to cough. It was infectious. I started laughing, too, and we couldn't stop.

CHAPTER THREE

NO MORE ASTERISKS

F all turkey hunting is like Minor League Baseball. Autumn birds count in your career statistics, but with asterisks.

Some of my most memorable hunts were in the fall, but spring hunting purists reject the legitimacy of autumn-killed turkeys. Some consider it unsporting because hunters in the fall often kill turkeys incidentally while hunting squirrels, rabbits, or upland birds. They stumble across a flock of jakes or hens, and if they have a tag or permit, they pot one. It often is a hen, which represents the loss of a bird that might have reproduced in the spring.

In some states, like Oklahoma and Nebraska, you can snipe turkeys in the fall with centerfire rifles. Such opportunistic scavenging reduces a turkey to a consolation prize, kind of like winning a carton of sodas for not knowing the count and the amount when "Dialing for Dollars" calls. Others reflexively assume that fall turkey seasons invite poaching and that the number of turkeys poached in the autumn far outpaces the number legally taken. These attitudes discredit a legitimate hunting genre, much to the dishonor of those that truly work at it.

That attitude enabled the Arkansas Game and Fish Commission to justify closing its fall turkey season in 2010. After a record spring harvest in 2003, turkey numbers declined precipitously, as did spring gobbler harvests. Although hunters only checked about 500 turkeys in the fall, the Game and Fish Commission believed that the statewide flock could not spare roughly seven turkeys per county.

Key factors in the decline were habitat degradation; cold, rainy weather during the hatching and brood-rearing season; overkilling of jakes; and loss of turkeys to predators like coyotes and bobcats. They, along with foxes, raccoons, skunks, opossums, owls, hawks, and crows, also eat untold numbers of turkey poults and eggs.

Advocates for closing fall turkey season, including those within the Game and Fish Commission, blamed hunting as a contributing factor. A majority of commissioners rationalized that squirrel and rabbit hunters killed turkeys opportunistically in the fall and speculated that they killed far more than they reported. This argument subtly stigmatized hunting as pernicious and undermined hunting's justification as a legitimate management tool. It was an irresponsible and divisive argument for a state agency to make against its largest, most loyal, and most politically active constituency.

Ultimately, the Game and Fish Commission closed fall turkey season by presenting closure as the last available regulatory tool to ease pressure on a struggling resource. In hindsight, it was the right thing to do on that basis. Fall hunting didn't hurt turkeys. Closing the fall season hurt them less.

My first turkey was a jake I killed in October 1999 in Roger Mills County, Oklahoma, while hunting with Danny Pierce, a guide from Reydon, and Steve DeMaso, the upland bird program coordinator for the Oklahoma Department of Wildlife Conservation.

Within minutes of our first hunt, DeMaso blew a few yelps on a diaphragm. He got busy putting out decoys and did not see the hen that skidded to a halt on the crest of a low hill in front of us. The hen quickly surveyed the scene, spun, and ran away before I could alert DeMaso.

That evening found us in a thicket of cedar and cottonwoods beside a creek. Flanked by Pierce and DeMaso, I called in a flock of about thirty-five Rio Grande turkeys. It was my first hunt with my new Winchester Model 1300 Black Shadow pump shotgun, a 12-gauge.

"Is that what you want to use?" Pierce asked, skeptically.

"It's what I have," I replied.

Pierce handed me his Remington 10-gauge semi-automatic.

"Now you'll know you did all you could do," he said, chuckling along with DeMaso.

The flock lingered on a ridge above the creek for so long that Pierce and DeMaso surrendered it to St. Jude. I continued scratching an HS Strut slate call. More turkeys joined the flock, swelling into a yelping, cackling mob. Finally, one turkey ventured down the slope into the creek bottom, and the rest of the flock followed in single file. Almost all were hens.

"You see a beard on any of them birds?" Pierce asked anxiously.

"That one right there looks like it has a beard, a really little one," I said.

"That's a jake. Kill him! Kill him!" Pierce hissed.

Turkeys spread skyward like smoke into a ceiling fan, but one bird flopped violently on the ground before hurling itself into the creek. Flailing the water with its wings, it was as good as dead, but in my excitement I fired another shot at its head from the top of the bank about ten feet above.

"Hey, hey, hey! Take it easy there, Buddy!" Pierce shouted as he and DeMaso raced to my side. "There won't be enough left to make a tender if you keep that up!"

Backslaps and laughter echoed through the thicket in the fading light as Pierce and DeMaso formally welcomed me into the turkey hunting brotherhood.

Soaked to my thighs in the plummeting cool of dusk, I retrieved the bird from the bloodstained creek. Pierce removed its breasts and stuffed them with ice into a large plastic freezer bag. I wrote my name, address, telephone number, and hunting license number on a strip of duct tape and wrapped it around the bird's leg so I could legally transport it home.

The jake's fan hangs over my office desk. With a jigsaw, my wife made the mount by cutting a piece of salvaged barn wood in the shape of Oklahoma. She painted the date of the kill in red. The dusty feather vanes have long separated and dulled to unsightliness, but I keep it because it was my first.

I killed my second turkey in the fall as well. It was a Missouri hen that was also part of a big flock on the same farm where I botched my first crack at a mature Eastern gobbler the previous April. I heard the turkeys clucking and scratching among dry leaves downhill from my position atop a low ridge. With a diaphragm, I clucked and made kee-kee calls for so long that my mouth parched. One hen finally came over the ridge to investigate.

I was proud of that hard-earned prize, but I was affronted when the attendant at the game check station grunted, "Hen bird," before slinging it onto his scale. His attitude represented the general disdain with which dedicated turkey hunters regard fall turkey hunting.

Nevertheless, I failed again to break into the major leagues in 2002, when the spring season ended on a spectacularly implausible note. I walked the entire farm that morning before sitting against a tree in a creek-bottom thicket. Having heard no turkeys, I blew loudly on a diaphragm every few minutes.

Instead of a turkey, I called up a deer. It stomped and snorted. I tried to ignore it, but the deer grew increasingly agitated. I flung a stick at it, offending it more. I leapt to my feet and lunged. The deer ran a few yards and then returned, protesting ever louder. Finally, I charged, swinging a big stick at the deer. That only convinced it to snort from a safer distance.

Thus began a pattern on that farm. I called up as many deer as turkeys, including a doe that poked her nose inside the branches of a downed tree that I used as a blind. I was sorely tempted to blow in her face, but I resisted, not knowing how she might react. The deer were always belligerent, and I almost always had to drive them off by throwing or swinging things at them.

After running off the aforementioned deer in the creek bottom, I sat back down and continued practicing with the diaphragm. With nothing to hold my attention, I started daydreaming about nothing in particular.

A tentative cluck jerked me back to consciousness. Just twenty yards away stood what appeared to be a two-year-old gobbler. The gobbler saw me flinch and hurried away. It was about 12:10 p.m. Turkey hunting in Missouri ends at 1 p.m. so that turkeys can breed and nest without hunters disrupting them. With fifty minutes left in the season, I trotted out in pursuit.

That part of the farm features a series of narrow pastures separated by wide cedar thickets that splay like fingers down a steep hill. Noting the gobbler's departure path, I crossed a creek bottom and scurried up the hill on a parallel path through a cedar thicket. I raced to the top of the hill to attain an ambush position at the head of its respective pasture. I clambered through one rusty barbed-wire fence and tore my pants on another. I nearly fell as I scrambled across slick, moist rocks.

Finally, I emerged at the top of the thicket and crossed the ridge to the head of the finger pasture through which I believed the gobbler was ascending. Panting and sweating, I found a tree big enough to cover my back, and I waited. About ten minutes later, I heard turkeys clucking as they came up the hill. The gobbler had picked up a hen or two, and they were drifting to me. With my shotgun on my knee, I fought to control my excitement.

The turkeys were less than a minute from cresting the ridge when a shadow flickered across the ground. I looked up and saw not a turkey, but a turkey vulture. Inexplicably, it banked hard and swooped low over the turkeys. They were only about sixty yards away but not yet in sight. The turkeys cackled, and then all was silent. The vulture scattered them, and the season ended without a chance of shooting.

As nature's vacuum cleaners, vultures fill a valuable niche by cleaning up the remains of the animal kingdom's lottery losers. It's the only time I've ever known one to save lives, but that vulture kept me in the minor leagues for one more season.

Like bookends, I killed my last fall turkey in Roger Mills County, Oklahoma, as well on Nov. 4, 2007. It also happened to be the first turkey ever killed by a modern hunter at Turley Ranch. The owner, Windle Turley, a prominent Dallas, Texas, attorney, invited me to be his first guest to hunt whitetails on his wondrous spread near Cheyenne, Oklahoma, not far from the Washita National Battlefield. Turley's property along the Washita River is where Lt. Col. George Custer mustered his troops on Nov. 27, 1868, to stage his infamous massacre of Cheyenne Chief Black Kettle's winter encampment, which is within the national battlefield property.

I ate dinner with Turley at his lodge the evening before my first hunt. Turley loves animals and said he preferred to run his ranch as a wildlife refuge, but wildlife biologists for the Oklahoma Department of Wildlife Conservation convinced him that he needed to cull some deer annually for the good of the herd and for the good of the habitat.

"Please don't take this the wrong way," Turley said. "I am really happy you're here, and I hope you have a wonderful time. You're welcome to anything I have here."

Turley paused and dabbed at the corner of his mouth with a napkin.

"But," he continued, his voice softening almost to a whisper as he leaned his face toward mine, "I hope the deer win."

After I killed a nine-point buck on the third day, my guide, Tony Sumpter, took me to an alfalfa field for a chance to kill a doe on the final day of my muzzleloader hunt.

"You might want to bring your shotgun in case we run into some turkeys," Sumpter said.

Turley Ranch teemed with Rio Grande turkeys. We encountered big flocks wherever we went. As we arrived at our field, two flocks occupied two different fields on the other side of the Washita River. After Sumpter and I established our deer hunting blind amid a row of Osage orange trees, Sumpter said that deer wouldn't begin entering the field for another two hours.

"If you want to try to get a turkey, now would be a good time," Sumpter said.

I returned to the truck for my Winchester Super X2 and noticed that the turkeys were migrating to the side of the field near the river. I would have to move quickly to establish a position in front of them.

A river in western Oklahoma is what passes for a creek in wetter climates. In the dry weather of November, the deepest holes are less than eighteen inches. To keep a low profile, I walked quickly through the creek to a spot where I believed the largest concentration of turkeys would enter the woods. I saw several turkeys flap across the Washita in the distance. Plowing forward, I maneuvered into a position that divided the flock. The group that already crossed the river dashed out of sight, causing the birds on the other side to grow anxious. I crouched as birds fluttered across the river in front of me. As I expected, one hen erred and came too close. One shot dropped her and put the rest of the turkeys to flight.

When I returned to the blind with a turkey slung over my shoulder, Sumpter was incredulous.

"I didn't hear you shoot," he said.

The dense river-bottom forest muffled the shot, hinting at how Custer's 7th Cavalry could advance undetected to the edge of a sprawling Native American settlement. I was proud of that hard-earned autumn bird, too, but it marked the end of my tenure in the minor leagues. A turkey hunter is judged by his springtime performances. I would launch my major league career in earnest five months later.

CHAPTER FOUR

THE IMMORTAL JAKE

I met Vernon Schmitz in April 2001 when his nephew invited me to hunt turkeys at Schmitz's farm near Jefferson City, Missouri. The nephew was even less experienced at turkey hunting than I was, but if it meant access to a prime piece of hunting property near the capital city, I was more than willing to fake the role of expert.

After an uneventful morning hunt, we broke for lunch and visited with Schmitz in his equipment shed. Schmitz, an auto mechanic in Jefferson City, took an immediate liking to me. We talked about classic muscle cars, tractors, deer, and deer rifles. Before we returned to the field for the afternoon hunt, Schmitz took me aside and told me that he didn't care a whit about turkey hunting, but I was welcome to hunt anytime, with or without the nephew.

Ironically, familiarizing myself with the property through deer hunting enabled me to experience some fabulous turkey hunts in subsequent years. I discovered all of the narrow funnels that wildlife use to travel among pastures, and I also learned the features within the hollows, especially a small web of seasonal creeks where turkeys travel in a similar fashion as deer.

In November 2001, I killed my first Missouri deer on Schmitz's farm. It was on a cold, clear November morning, and I sat on a high point overlooking a long pasture that stretched the length of a hilltop. The pasture ended at a woodlot where, in May 2004, I killed my last Missouri gobbler before moving back home to Arkansas and also where my turkey hunt with Schmitz's nephew ended with incandescent failure.

Late in the morning of the deer hunt, a large herd of deer emerged from the wooded bottom below the south side of the field, but they filtered back into the woods before I could identify a buck. They returned about fifteen minutes later, and a young buck showed me a broadside profile. One shot with a Winchester Model 70 Classic Featherweight dropped the deer at about 200 yards with one of my own hand-loaded 308 Winchester cartridges. The bullet struck with a resounding thud, knocking the deer down with astonishing authority. The violence of the impact was awesome and sobering, and it heightened my reverence for the terminal act of hunting.

Mere moments before, the deer was content in his business, oblivious to the onrush of kinetic energy that would see the remainder of a splendid autumn morning mature without him. He was too young to have sired children, and too young even to have grown antlers that would have provided scant physical evidence of his brief existence. His life was but a vapor, and after the last of his venison was consumed, he might as well have never existed. Some deer live long and flourish, distributing their genes over generations. Others leave this realm suddenly and violently, depending solely on the random convergence of time, space, and circumstance.

After retrieving the deer with his tractor, Schmitz showed me how to open a deer's pelvis and rib cage with a hatchet and a small sledgehammer. This makes it much easier and much cleaner to remove a deer's organs. Then, Schmitz stuffed several zip-close bags of ice inside the deer's body cavity and closed the body cavity by tying twine tightly around the chest. This cools the body from the inside and helps ensure good venison flavor.

The nearest check station was at a city park pavilion in the town of Linn. A crabby old woman ran the check station. Her wiry hair reminded me of tangled fishing line, and her voice was a cigarette-ravaged growl. Her husband astutely kept out of her way. The woman looked at the address on my hunting license and asked icily, "What'sa matter? Ain't y'all got no deer over where you live?"

"Yes, ma'am, we've got lots of deer," I replied airily, "but I'd rather come over here and shoot some of yours."

It was like the moment when a villain swaggers into the saloon in a western movie. Traffic stopped on the highway. Birds quit singing. The breeze stilled. The woman glared holes through my skull while her lips gripped the filter of a smoldering cigarette. She dragged the nib of her ink pen so hard against her deer checkbook that I thought she might rip the paper.

Her husband stood behind her, shoulders heaving, trying to stifle laughter. Knowing there would be hell to pay when she got done with me, he ducked out the back of the pavilion for his own private smoke break. The woman followed me to my truck, clipped a transportation tag on my deer, and shuffled back to the pavilion.

"That all you need from me?" I chirped.

She did not answer nor break stride.

Thanks in part to Schmitz's vast knowledge about hunting and his deep familiarity with every fold and crag on his property, I learned a great deal about hunting deer and, later, wild turkeys on the farm.

Schmitz never plainly told me where to find turkeys. Instead, he casually mentioned having seen turkeys roosting in a certain grove in a remote corner or having seen turkeys on a particular hillside in the afternoon. The timing of these sightings was always vague, and Schmitz mentioned them almost in passing. It took me a while to realize that he only mentioned turkeys when his information was current.

As the nephew and I finished our lunch in Schmitz's equipment shed during our first meeting, a turkey gobbled in a nearby hollow. We hurried to the far end of the field where we had left our decoy standing at the edge of the woods. Sitting shoulder to shoulder, I faced out to the field, and my companion faced the woods. I yelped and clucked with my mouth call, but we heard no more gobbles.

"Keep sharp because that gobbler could pop out of that hollow just about anywhere," I whispered.

"There's a turkey right in front of me," my companion whispered in reply. "I'm pretty sure that's a gobbler."

Only then did I notice that my companion had removed his camouflage sweatshirt. With only his gray T-shirt and winter-white arms, he was as bright as a Broadway debut. I jerked my head around to see a mature, long-bearded gobbler inspecting us from about twenty yards away. The movement spurred the gobbler to dash into the brush, putt-putting loudly.

"What is your problem?" I demanded.

"What!?" my companion asked.

"Man, a turkey can see you from a mile away! Why did you take off your camo?"

"I got hot," my companion replied meekly.

Opening day of the 2001 fall turkey season brought me back to Schmitz's farm. After a dry summer, the creeks hold water only in a few deep pools separated by long expanses of dry gravel. The creek beds are about five feet below the banks. Deer and turkeys travel through the ravine with the gentler grade because it offers plenty of concealed access points into the fields. It also conceals them as they traverse the farm to a neighboring farm across the highway.

Fall turkey season in Missouri coincides with the onset of the rutting season for white-tailed deer, so deer are very active on cool October mornings. Waiting for turkeys, I watched a pair of young bucks with spindly spike antlers sparring playfully, doing little more than butting heads. When they matured, they would sport formidable antlers with tall, sharp tines. These playful shoving matches would then become hormone-fueled, no-holds-barred battles for breeding dominance.

About a week later at the Missouri Department of Conservation headquarters in Jefferson City, for example, a member of a line crew repairing an electrical service called the office early one morning and reported that two bucks were fighting near his bucket truck.

"They're going at it like nobody's business," he said. "You might be able to get some good pictures if somebody can get down here real quick."

Jim Rathert, our photographer, hurried down the hill and captured the final moments of the battle. Two mature bucks stood in a creek, locked in mortal, antler-to-antler combat. One buck had slightly smaller antlers, but its body was bigger and heavier. It forced the other buck's head underwater and held it submerged until the opponent drowned. It disengaged from the dead buck and looked at Rathert aggressively, prompting Rathert to seek protective cover. Hackles bristling, the buck marched stiff-legged into the woods. We published the photos as a mini-essay in *Missouri Conservationist* magazine.

While reckless aggression makes white-tailed bucks vulnerable to hunters in the fall, wild turkey gobblers are reclusive and secretive at that time. When hunting turkeys in the fall, one usually sees hens or jakes. The classic hunting technique is to charge into a flock of jakes and disperse the birds by firing three shots. Fire twice rapidly, hesitate, and then discharge the third shell. That's the one that really scatters the birds. The jakes are anxious to reassemble, and they will eagerly come to a sequence of plaintive squealing yelps known as the "kee-kee-run."

Yelping on a diaphragm at Schmitz's farm during the 2002 fall turkey season, I saw movement flicker through a gap in the trees on a gravel flat beside the creek. I saw another flicker, and then another. About fifteen jakes had gathered on the flat. When one bird separated from the others, I flattened him with one shot from the same Winchester 1300 pump-action 12-gauge that Danny Pierce replaced with a 10-gauge Remington when I killed my first turkey in Oklahoma.

The other jakes jumped on the flailing jake, pecking and pummeling it mercilessly. I charged into the fracas to subdue my bird while the other jakes stood stupefied. I could have swung my gun by the barrel and hit five or six of them.

Like a resilient hero in an action thriller, my stricken jake leapt to its feet and sped toward cover as I prepared to plant my foot on his neck. Off balance, I fired twice and missed, causing all of the other turkeys to scatter.

Having spent all of my ammo, I ran up the hill to my truck and stuffed half a box of shells in my vest. Panting from exertion, I hurriedly devised a strategy to salvage the hunt. From deep in the hollow, I heard several kee-kee calls emanating from the tree branches. The flock was still in play, but I had to hasten back to the hollow before the jakes returned to the ground and reassembled.

The hollow was quiet when I finally arrived. I returned to the spot where I last saw my stricken jake and visualized his last known route into the woods. Knowing that wounded birds sometimes nestle into protective cover, I crisscrossed the flat looking under every downed tree and into every briar thicket. Emerging from the thicket into the dry creek, I spied a dark mass in the recess of an undercut bank. It was my jake, huddled in a crease beneath a root wad behind a web of overhanging vines.

"Ohhh, I've got you now," I murmured with a menacing chuckle.

Squaring my feet, I aimed at the jake's compact head and neck area and squeezed the trigger. The report still echoed when the jake rocketed out of the recess. The vines parted as he flew over the creek bed and made a sharp, climbing turn. I fired again as the jake gained speed and altitude, and I fired my third shot at his rear as he cleared the trees and flapped midway across the opposite pasture before setting his wings and gliding to distant woods.

Marking the spot where I last saw him, I trudged across the field and searched for about forty minutes in woods that had no prominent places for a turkey to hide. I looked among large, low tree branches in case the jake had sought refuge overhead, but I found no sign of him. If he continued aground on his flight path, he crossed the highway onto the adjacent farm to which I didn't have permission to enter.

Livid, I marched back to my truck and drove straight to Boggs Creek Gun Shop in Jefferson City. Kern Robins, the store owner, was a member of my skeet shooting team at the United Sportsmen's Club. He greeted me warmly but quickly grew defensive when he sensed my ire.

"I'll take whatever you give me for this shotgun," I said, placing the Winchester on his counter, action open.

"What's wrong with it?" Robins asked suspiciously, backing slightly away from the counter.

"What's wrong with it is it won't kill a damn turkey sitting still twenty-five feet away," I fumed.

Robins relaxed and listened with reserved amusement as I relived the morning's misadventures.

"I can break little clay targets in flight with a tiny little 28-gauge all day long, but I'll miss a sixteen-pound turkey at point-blank range with this big-ass twelve! I hate this frickin' gun! I'll take whatever you give me for it. I just want it gone."

Of course the gun wasn't to blame, but that was the second gimme turkey I'd missed, and it had gotten in my head. I had come to expect missing, and that attitude prevents success. The gun and I were incompatible, and our partnership could not continue. It was like a team owner firing a coach after an emotional loss. It's irrational and impulsive, but a faulty equation is the product of at least one faulty variable. The gun was the radical variable. I was stuck with myself, but the gun was expendable. Robins gave me a fair price, and I replaced that gun with a Winchester Super X2 semi-automatic 12-gauge that I bought months later during a trip to Oklahoma City to shoot photos for a *Bassmaster Magazine* article about smallmouth bass fishing at Lake Lawtonka.

The swap was momentous, like trading an error-prone quarterback for a future all-star. Winchester must have designed the Super X2 with me as a template. It replicated the graceful lines of its predecessor, the beloved but short-lived Super X1, with a simplified gas compensating action. Unlike the X1, which could only chamber 2 ¾-inch shells, the X2 chambered three-inch and 3 ½-inch shells. Unlike other shotguns with 3 ½-inch chambers, the X2 reliably cycles the heaviest magnum loads as well as light target loads. It fit me perfectly, and it was one of the best shotguns I ever owned. Whether hunting turkeys, ducks, geese, or woodcocks, it never missed. It was the missing ingredient that turned me into a winner.

CHAPTER FIVE

BUDDHA

Buddha roosted in a tree at the edge of a bluff overlooking a field that bordered the Lamine River at the Lamine River Conservation Area (CA) near Tipton, Missouri.

Lamine River CA, a vast collection of grain fields, hardwoods, woody fencerows, wetlands, and river bottoms, is my favorite public hunting area in Missouri. I killed my first antlered buck there, and it is an outstanding place to hunt woodcocks. If you look hard enough, there are also some excellent places to hunt ducks.

My last Missouri quail hunt was at Lamine River. In an early-winter gale, I flushed a small covey that raced to a distant brush row. One bird got too high and stalled against a wind wall. It flapped furiously in place until it tired and tumbled backward. I ran under it like an outfielder shagging a fly ball and caught the bird with my hands before releasing it in a thicket. Catching quail is not a prescribed method of taking in Missouri, and although it was a once-in-a-lifetime catch, killing a quail taken in such a manner would be unsporting.

Having encountered no birds at the end of another Lamine River quail hunt in early November, I contemplated the state of my ancient 16-gauge ammunition, which I bought from a member of my skeet team who had kept it in his garage for thirty years.

I wonder if this stuff even works, I thought.

Of course it worked. The question merely rationalized shooting my gun after uneventful hours of walking through brushy, weedy cover. With the sun setting, I fired a shot from my Browning Sweet Sixteen from behind my truck toward an adjoining field. I watched dumbstruck as about twenty bobwhites erupted from a ditch and rocketed to the safety of a nearby woodlot.

That incident was analogous to my turkey hunting career at Lamine River, where eccentricity was normal. Never was it more evident than on a spring turkey hunt in 2003 with my friend Derrick Harmon, a sales representative for a company that printed *Missouri Conservationist* magazine, for which I was managing editor. Harmon was a superb turkey hunter and an enthusiastic mentor.

We arrived before dawn and entered a thin patch of woods that ended at a bluff. We did not know that a giant gobbler roosted in a gnarled tree at the edge of the bluff, so we were gobsmacked when the bird burst from the tree amid a thrashing of leaves, cracking branches, and staccato wing thumps. We plopped to the ground with the vain hope of calling the gobbler back to that spot. He probably abandoned that roost for good, but I called up a hen that came so close behind me that I felt the vibrations of her throaty purrs tingle against my nape. It wasn't the usual contented purr that you hear from a distance. It was more like a cat's purr, deep and rumbling. The hen turned to depart, but I called her back, and we repeated the encounter. Eventually, the hen left for the field below as well.

Harmon, who witnessed the encounter from about five yards away, said, "I thought she was going to peck your ear!"

"I thought so too," I said. "I braced for it, but I'd have filled my shorts if she'd done it!"

In my shotgun's present configuration, I can kill a turkey at fifty yards, but I won't. So electrifying was that experience that my goal from that moment was to call birds into my lap. I not only want to hear a gobbler spit and drum but also to feel it. I want the scrape of his wingtips in the leaves to make my skin crawl. I want to see his crimson wattles pulse and glow. I want to see indigo flood across his pale head. I crave the melting of my insides when he cuts loose a rebel yell. It's like a drug to me. I can't get enough of it. If I can't call a gobbler close enough to torch my senses, I don't deserve him.

Morning progressed, and there were clearly no more turkeys on the hill. Harmon and I eased toward the edge of the bluff and scanned the field below through binoculars. Eight or nine hens foraged contentedly among rows of cut milo, but every few minutes, a hen stood erect and then dashed to the edge of the field.

"What's spooking those hens?" I asked. "There's no way they can see us that far away, especially with us in camo under all these trees."

When the next hen bolted, we followed her with our binoculars. In tall grass at the edge of the field stood a giant gobbler in full display, shiny and smug amid his adoring harem. In order of rank, the hens ran to him one by one to be bred. He was the only gobbler in the field, so we were certain he was the one we spooked off the bluff.

Behind the gobbler was a strip of woods abutting the Lamine River. The river protected Buddha from behind, and the clear view of the field protected him from the front. His throne was unapproachable without early detection. Buddha was obviously an old gobbler, and he picked his breeding ground well.

I never saw Buddha again. After the close encounter on the bluff, he probably relocated to a different part of the area.

Even though I didn't bag Buddha, the experience was my first major lesson on how to pattern an old gobbler. Like mature white-tailed bucks, king birds like Buddha seldom venture far from protective cover, and when they do, they minimize their exposure.

That's one of the few blanket characterizations I assign to a wild turkey, and it's one of the most valuable lessons of my career. To harvest a bird of that caliber, you must infiltrate citadels that deter nature's most efficient predators, and you must get there before the gobbler does, no matter how early you must rise to do it.

I tried to infiltrate Buddha's citadel one more time that season, but Buddha's pawn row made it a very costly incursion. About four hours after that hunt ended, I felt an intense itch on the right underside of my wrist. It was a lone star tick, indistinguishable from dozens I've encountered, solidly embedded. I pulled it loose with an audible pop, placed it in a teaspoon and roasted it over a gas flame on my kitchen range. My mother-in-law taught me this method of execution. She was frugal in all other matters, but she gladly splurged on a little natural gas to roast a tick. That was a mistake on my part. I should have put the tick in a bag and frozen it. Having it intact would have been useful.

About a week later, I got feverish, with night sweats. That was odd because flu season had long passed, and nobody in my orbit had been ill since winter. The symptoms abated but returned about a week later and lasted a little longer. They abated anew but recurred with greater intensity and duration.

I was in the washroom at work when I saw in the mirror a large, bull's-eye-shaped rash around the site of the tick bite.

"Well, son of a gun," I said softly.

I returned to my office and promptly called my doctor.

"I think I have Lyme disease," I said.

The doctor was understandably skeptical because Missouri at that point had not had a documented case of the dreaded tick-borne illness. I described the rash and symptoms, and the doctor summoned me to his office immediately.

"Well, son of a gun," the doctor said softly, rolling my arm forward and backward, inspecting it from multiple angles. He called in the rest of the clinic staff and said, "Here's what it looks like."

"That doesn't make any sense, Doc," I said. "All of the literature says a tick has to be attached for thirty-six to forty-eight hours to transmit Lyme disease. This tick was attached for only about four hours."

"Well, apparently you're an exception to the literature," the doctor said.

He prescribed massive doses of doxycycline, and I had no more problems. I did, however, report it to the Missouri Health Department. At least, I tried to report it. The bureaucrat that took my call demanded complete documentation.

"What kind of documentation?" I asked.

"Documentation in the form of a lab report that confirms you had Lyme disease because Lyme disease does not exist in Missouri," she said haughtily.

Since I could produce no such documentation, the State of Missouri was able to continue making that claim for a while longer. The bureaucrat sounded positively giddy to cheat me out of my rightful place in state history.

In addition to accentuating the benefits of tick repellent, Buddha exposed the shortcomings of hunting an area without advance reconnaissance. Eventide scouting might have revealed Buddha's roosting place on the bluff, and daytime observations might have revealed his daily glide to his little parlor by the river. Scouting would have enabled me to greet him. Failing to scout put me at a disadvantage because Buddha was always one move ahead of me. That lesson paid rich dividends in later years when hunting large public areas where other gobblers of Buddha's stature didn't fare as well.

CHAPTER SIX

THE ICEBREAKER

Beginning with some of my earliest turkey hunts, I developed a careless habit of busting gobblers on the roost as I walked to my hunting spots. While the chance of blundering into a turkey is statistically remote, I try to minimize opportunities for freak encounters by taking routes through areas where turkeys shouldn't roost. However, gobblers must seek those areas to minimize freak encounters with hunters because those are precisely where I often encounter them.

Conventionally, I could break that habit by scouting. Principally, I agree, but scouting is problematic when you live fifty miles from your hunting spot. If you work a nine-to-five job, that means going directly to the woods after work on curvy, narrow country roads and getting home long after the family has eaten dinner and the kids are preparing for bed. It is seldom practical, and it disrupts domestic harmony. Even when you have the time to scout, turkeys can change roost locations overnight for any number of reasons. It happens a lot in the woods where I hunt.

Ordinarily, I stay out of the woods as the season nears to avoid any chance of bumping turkeys in daylight. Turkeys are especially sensitive to pressure in the small tracts of mature pines on my hunting lease. If I bump turkeys, they might not return for the rest of the season. On public areas, people looking for shed deer antlers, morels, and wild onions unknowingly disrupt turkey patterns as well. In similar fashion, many hunters bump turkeys while scouting, mainly because they cannot resist calling.

We can't help ourselves. Even though we wouldn't dare kill a turkey out of season, we crave live drills with gobblers. We enter the woods intending only to listen, but turkey hunters are gregarious folks who consider it rude to spurn polite conversation, especially with a gobbler whose opinion we value. If we hear a gobble, we must reply, if for no other reason but to see what happens next. And what do we believe will happen? All turkey hunters expect a reply. The gobbler believes he must have the last word, but so must we.

Once the conversation begins, naturally we must see how the gobbler rates. We want to see his beard. We want to estimate his weight. If he has companion gobblers, we want to evaluate them too. At this point we are no longer scouting but taking inventory, and we may well have already compromised our mission.

To prevent such an encounter, some of us scout in the afternoon because many of us believe turkeys evaporate at 10 a.m. We delude ourselves into believing that we shall not encounter turkeys where we expect to have encountered them at dawn. We seek not sound, but evidence in the form of droppings, feathers, tracks, and dusting areas. We examine turkey scat and turkey tracks, both for freshness. Scat gives us other clues, such as an elongated shape and characteristic J-hook of a gobbler dropping. We examine it for moisture. Moist scat was deposited recently. We often roll it over with a stick, as if the poo is trying to fool us. Different degrees of dryness give us a clue as to how long ago the gobbler deposited it. We try to divine the meaning contained within degrees of dryness, examining grain, texture, and hue with an art critic's eye.

Ultimately, however, we often yield to temptation. Having gleaned all we can from physical evidence, we seek confirmation by casting a wider net. Many turkey hunters, especially the inexperienced, bring at least a diaphragm to a scouting expedition. Silence unnerves them. It saps their confidence in a spot. A gobble justifies their decision to scout this spot, so they seek feedback. They call. Not much, just a few yelps.

If a gobbler responds, he will come looking for the source of the call. It is merely practice for the scout, but not to a gobbler. His sole desire is to make little baby turkeys, and if you convince him that you're a willing partner, you have again compromised your mission. If you spook him, the gobbler will associate the tone and cadence of your call with danger. Turkey hunters call that "educating" a gobbler.

If he doesn't find you, he might associate the sound of your call with a hen that he couldn't find. Mating is urgent business. A gobbler hasn't time for hens he can't find. We would avoid all of this if we would just be quiet.

In the woods that I hunt year after year, I know where turkeys ought to be. I know where they usually roost, where they usually go after leaving the roost, and where they usually go in the midmornings, late mornings, and afternoons. I know every game trail, and I know every intersection that leads to the middle and the edges of my woods. I know all of the high areas where turkeys prefer to roost, and I avoid them in the dark. Even so, I roust at least one bird out of a roost every other year. That doesn't sound like a bad ratio at face value, but believe me, it breaks my heart every time it happens.

One notable roost eviction occurred on opening day of the 2002 spring season at a farm in Miller County, Missouri, near the Osage River. As I ascended the top of a ridge, a bird launched from a tree in the gathering dawn. Logic suggested that any place a gobbler roosts must be a good place to hunt. Furthermore, logic suggested that a gobbler should return to a good place. Maybe that particular gobbler won't come back, but another surely will.

We turkey hunters often plant our flags on untenable logic, but that line of hasty reasoning prompted me to plant my rear against the nearest big tree. Coincidentally, it was very near the spot where I called up two gobblers while scouting two days before encountering a mature bird that I missed as a result of failing to pattern my shotgun. I concluded that it was an exceptional spot.

Turkeys did not race to my calls, but I did call up yet another deer that I had to chase off with a stick. The dance featured all the familiar steps. I flailed my arms, and the deer sprinted a few yards away before returning in a snorting fit. I chunked a rock at it, which provoked it to come closer and snort and stomp louder. The final act was, of course, to stagger upright, grab a limb, and chase the deer.

To my astonishment, the commotion attracted a gobbler that may have mistaken all the thrashing for two turkeys fighting. The gobbler bellowed close but out of sight, and I soon learned two more valuable lessons. Although I made decent sounds with a mouth call, I had not yet learned to modulate pitch or volume. When a gobbler is close, you should call quietly and sparingly. You should also direct sound to the ground and away from the gobbler to vary direction. The gobbler was aroused, and eventually he would have come to investigate. A few light purrs and clucks would have sufficed. Many accomplished turkey hunters insist that even that is too much and that you should remain silent in that situation.

Instead, I wailed on that diaphragm as if I were playing a jazz solo. The gobbler went silent, but I did not. I mistakenly believed that the gobbler would stroll straight down my sonic runway. The gobbler did not come. After many minutes of an unrequited serenade, I got discouraged and did precisely what I should not have done. I stood. Once on my feet, I saw the backside of a gobbler running away. He had watched from a distance the whole time, looking for a hen whose volume indicated immediate proximity.

I was crestfallen, and my confidence was shattered. It's easy in retrospect to see that all my early self-inflicted wounds were products of inexperience. Self-education is taxing for a career student in the college of hard knocks, but at the time I wondered if I would ever kill a spring gobbler. It certainly didn't help to concede that most of my mistakes were also the results of simple stupidity. Self-recrimination led me to acknowledge repeatedly that I was an incorrigibly bad hunter.

I continued up the ridge and promptly walked headlong into two more gobblers that were probably coming to investigate my hideously loud hen noises. From a long distance, my calls probably sounded pretty good to them. It was a classic lose-lose proposition. Anything I did that morning was bound to be wrong.

Disheartened, I emerged from the woods into a sun-drenched glade at the top of the ridge. Tall, golden grass swayed gently in the soft morning breeze, and freshly minted oak and hickory foliage whispered calming reassurance. For me, that kind of place triggers an irresistible urge to sit. Such an idyll lured Rip Van Winkle to his twenty-year slumber. Eric Burdon sang about it in War's "Spill the Wine." It liberated Rip from an abusive marriage and plied Burdon with satyric delights. Maybe it portended something nice for me as well.

The glade's warmth and the saturated morning light were like reassuring hands on my troubled shoulder. Had I skirted that ridgetop, I might have walked out of the field and away from turkey hunting forever. Something that causes that much heartache isn't worth the angst. It's kind of like being in a star-crossed love affair. The passion and excitement are irresistibly combustible, but drama and disappointment ultimately bitter the sweet.

Such were my thoughts when I sat against an old wooden fencepost. This constituted yet another tactical error. I was in direct sunlight. I shone as bright as a brand new car, but I didn't care. My hunt was finished for the day. I just wanted to savor a few glorious moments in a new place that I probably wouldn't see again.

And since I was there, it would be a sin not to work a turkey call.

I pulled a slate out of my vest, extracted a striker from its pouch, and dragged it across the surface five times. "Yee-awp, yawp, yawp, yawp, yawp!" It sounded good, and I liked the gritty sensation vibrating through the striker stem, so I did it again. Sensing a presence, I looked up. Three jakes stood staring a mere twenty-five yards away! Naturally, I was unprepared. My shotgun lay across my lap. My left hand held the call, and my right hand held the striker.

"Give me just one second, boys," I said softly.

I slowly put the slate and striker on the ground, hoisted my Winchester Super X2 from my lap, and shot a jake that stood apart from the other two. In a blink, depression became elation.

From 2000–05, I was managing editor for *Missouri Conservationist* magazine, the official publication of the Missouri Department of Wildlife Conservation. We had recently published an article written by Mark Goodwin titled, "Just a Jake." Goodwin argued that killing a one-year-old gobbler is a worthy accomplishment, especially for young and novice hunters. If a jake is good enough for as fine a hunter as Goodwin, then it was good enough for me.

My journey to that point was analogous to my early attempts in the 1990s trying to break into the freelance magazine writing business. Editors rejected every query, often rudely. I took it personally, oblivious to the amateurism of my early attempts, but I kept punching away, refining my pitch and noting what did and did not resonate with editors. I learned to target my pitches to their specific needs. When I finally sold my first piece, the puzzle magically came together. From that point on, assignments far outpaced rejections.

Fittingly, my own "Just a Jake" hunt produced the script for my first freelance turkey hunting article. The storyline went like this: "An inexperienced hunter lucked into an inexperienced turkey, and for once the turkey made the decisive error. The clouds parted, and the sun beamed down on the hard-luck protagonist who triumphed over adversity."

After thanking the Good Lord, I thanked Mark Goodwin as I attached a tag to my first spring gobbler.

Chapter Seven

TIGER DAN

S pringtime in Missouri is the tear of compassion that restored humanity to Kai's jaded eyes in Hans Christian Andersen's *The Snow Queen.*

Bitter cold arrives in late November, bringing waves of ice and snow that deepen weekly. This Arkansas boy learned to love it, especially the nights of long, moonlit walks in the snow with my kids and dog. The reverse monochrome created a celluloid negative effect and brought an ethereal dimension to nocturnal games of hide-and-seek in which my dog, with her keen nose, had an unfair advantage.

Missourians hunt in the snow and fish through the ice. We even get faint flashes of the aurora borealis, but always we gaze ahead to spring. Dogwoods and redbuds carpet the hillsides in pastel quilts of white and purple. Fields and pastures are lush and green, twinkling with suggestive winks from coquettish wildflowers. On warm, moist mornings, morels pop up at field edges and in damp hollows, often around rotting ash logs in mayapple groves. We gather them furtively but share with friends and neighbors. Stir-fried in butter with wild onions, wild garlic, squash, and sweet peas, morels are God's gift to gatherers.

Spring's scent is that of newborn nature. Like line-dried laundry, it wafts renewal and hope. We lived through winter. We live for spring, when streams teem with smallmouth bass, goggle-eyes, and trout. The headline act, of course, is the fan dance of the Eastern wild turkey.

My son Daniel, then age 10, was homeschooled during Missouri's 2004 spring turkey season. Spring fever made the chronically distracted student intractable. As his principal and superintendent, I issued a day pass for a turkey hunt at a friend's farm in Miller County. We camped on-site, and the extra hour of sleep allowed us to rise fresh for the dawn.

Daniel sipped a mug of hot chocolate, and I sipped coffee, both made from water boiled atop a Coleman stove on my truck's tailgate. We each ate half a honeybun for breakfast before donning our gear and making the long walk in the dark to Jake Ridge, where I killed my first spring gobbler two years earlier. It was Daniel's first turkey hunt, and while he did not understand my infatuation with the sport, he was happy to be out of the house and out from under his mother's apron strings for a day afield with "popster."

The second of my seven children, Daniel took his first breath in the same living room where his older brother, Ethan, was born two years earlier. One month later, Daniel contracted pneumonia and fell deathly ill in the night. He was clinically dead when he arrived at the hospital, but divine intervention and heroic medical attention revived him. After eleven days in intensive care, he returned home.

Though a frail and delicate toddler, Daniel was indomitable, with a lion's courage and a leopard's ferocity. While visiting the Little Rock Zoo, Daniel demanded that his cousin lower him into the tiger enclosure.

"I'm gonna ride that tiger!" he declared.

From then on, he was "Tiger Dan."

On the back of our detached garage at our California, Missouri, home was an empty room that my boys used as a clubhouse. On one corner was a vent covered by a steel grate. Two neighbor boys came for a weekend sleepover, and they adjourned to the clubhouse for a night of conspiratorial adventure. I crept across the yard and listened through the grate as they told horrific stories about axe murderers, slashers, and chainsaw butchers. At the conclusion of one particularly gruesome tale, I wailed mournfully and slammed my hand against the grate. The boys fell deathly quiet. After a dramatic pause, I contorted my hand into a claw and scraped my fingertips down the grate with an anguished moan.

One of the neighbor boys screamed. His brother cried out for his mother.

"It's a monster!" shouted my son Ethan.

"Let's kill it!" yelled Daniel.

Aluminum ball bats scraped against the concrete floor as the boys scurried for the door amid a chorus of bloodthirsty shouts. I fled across the yard in the dark, vaulted the gate, and escaped down the driveway before the mob rounded the garage corner.

Daniel was a mediocre student, but his keen street sense more than compensated for his academic indifference. In a room of strangers, he could instantly distinguish the sincere from the spurious, the honest from the dishonest, and the authentic from the inauthentic. He liked or disliked you instantly. Either way, it was for life.

Like his father, Daniel lived to be outdoors. Afield or adrift, we shed the customary yin and yang of the father-son relationship, and he thrived in the one arena where men and boys are equals. When he was small, I told him, "If you can talk authoritatively about guns, shooting, and hunting, grown men from all walks of life will listen to what you have to say." He took my advice to heart and earned the respect of men he respected.

In early 2005, for example, Daniel and I joined a group of avid quail hunters for a weekend in the Ouachita National Forest of western Arkansas. All of the men worked for the U.S. Forest Service, including Warren Montague, a wildlife biologist who engineered the Pine-Bluestem Restoration Project to reestablish the endangered red-cockaded woodpecker to the westernmost part of its native range. The Pine-Bluestem Restoration Project paid an unexpected dividend by sparking a resurgence of other wildlife, including bob-white quail. Consequently, the rugged highlands of the Ouachita National Forest support some of the largest numbers of wild bob-white quail in the Southeast as well as some of the largest turkey populations in western Arkansas.

Our relationship started professionally in 1996 when I was a young reporter for the *Southwest Times-Record* in Fort Smith, Arkansas. Montague took me on a tour of the project area during its genesis and explained the finer points of restoring native shortleaf pine-bluestem savannas that dominated the landscape when indigenous people inhabited that country. I accompanied him afield as he released red-cockaded woodpeckers that had been trapped in Texas and Louisiana.

As our professional relationship evolved into friendship, Montague demonstrated the recreational fruits of the Pine-Bluestem Restoration Project by taking me quail hunting. I documented the project's success locally, regionally, and nationally in magazine articles, bringing valuable recognition to an unknown facet of a chronically underfunded and unappreciated agency.

Montague shaped the way I cover conservation and environmental subjects by teaching me the intricate relationship between humans, wildlife, and the importance of aggressively manipulating habitat. Native Americans groomed the landscape to increase game-animal populations long before European migrants arrived. Game animals, especially quail and wild turkeys, flourished in the checkerboard landscape of small family farms after European migrants displaced indigenous people. Quail populations crashed in the late 1900s when large public and private landowners converted vast acreages to even-age pine plantations and imprinted the dogma of fire suppression on the American psyche. The use of prescribed fire is an essential element of forest management in the Ouachita National Forest. It contributes mightily to the abundance of game and non-game animals, as well as native flora, and it also greatly reduces the threat of wildfire.

"We still love Smokey Bear," said Joe Neal, Montague's assistant, "but we also want the public to get to know Smokey's cousin, Burnie Bear."

Resourceful and imaginative, the idiosyncratic Montague spurned convention in his relentless quest for results, but his contrarian streak extended afield as well. For example, upland bird hunters traditionally prefer pointing dog breeds like setters, spaniels, and English pointers. Many contemporary hunters use multi-purpose dogs like Labrador retrievers and drahthaars. Montague was famous for hunting with a wire-haired terrier named Moxie, whom I honored posthumously in *Quail Forever* magazine. His favorite shotgun was a Ruger Red Label over/under 20-gauge, an early version with a blued receiver instead of the Red Label's signature nickel finish.

"Everybody teases me about my 20-gauge shotgun and my .410-gauge dog," Montague quipped.

Late in the last day of our 2005 hunt in the Ouachita National Forest, two bird dogs pointed over a fallen log at the edge of a thicket.

Daniel hadn't gotten to shoot, so we sent him to engage the covey alone while the rest of the group watched from a distance. Instead of quail, a small owl burst from the cover. We all watched in horror, helpless to prevent Daniel from shooting a federally protected species. Everyone except me was a federal employee, but I worked for a state wildlife management agency. We all shouted and waved our arms, but Daniel was too far away to hear us in time to react.

Daniel snapped his shotgun to his shoulder and swung on the fleeing owl, but then he calmly retracted his shotgun to port arms and looked at us, puzzled.

"It ain't a quail!" he yelled.

The group exhaled a collective sigh of relief and greeted Daniel with cheers and back slaps when he returned.

"You've got a sharp eye and some damned fine self-control, young man," Montague gushed. "You're welcome to hunt in my camp anytime!"

Daniel beamed, basking in the approval of these gruff, veteran hunters.

Upon completing their elementary grades in a homeschool environment, my children were educated in the traditional fashion, but Daniel's practical education occurred under my tutelage. He often shadowed me in my work, and he especially enjoyed accompanying me to cover the Bassmaster Classic bass fishing championship tournament. Our first was the 2008 Classic at Greenville, South Carolina. The Bassmaster Classic media corps worked frenetically during the event, and fourteen-year-old Daniel was always at my side as I interviewed anglers exiting the weigh-in stage. He ran errands and acted as my liaison with the event staff.

We spent our nights in the company of the "Fun Bunch," the core of which was a group of Chicagoans that assisted Doug Grassian,

BASS's chief publicist and event coordinator. The unofficial leader of the Fun Bunch was Chauncey Niziol, a loud, profane, and charismatic Chicago radio personality. At dinner on the first night of the event, Niziol sat across the table from Daniel, who made no attempt to disguise his disdain for the garrulous Northerner. Delighted, Niziol peppered Daniel with questions as if he were interviewing a guest on his radio program.

"Speak up!" Niziol barked. "I can't understand that hillbilly accent of yours over all this damn noise!"

Daniel deeply resented rural southern stereotypes. "Go local, go yokel," was one of his maxims. Niziol's teasing galled Daniel, and he fumed all the way back to our hotel.

At dinner the next night, Niziol again sat across from Daniel and said, "I'm glad your old man brought you back because I've got some more questions to ask you!"

By the end of that dinner, Daniel's resistance crumbled. Niziol only teased those he liked. The rest he ignored. It was Niziol's way of initiating Daniel as an honorary member of the Fun Bunch, without full privileges, of course, because of Dan's age. On the eve of every Bassmaster Classic thereafter, Daniel always lit up when he discovered "that Chauncey guy" would be there.

At lunch during the Greenville Classic, Daniel and I ate at the Sticky Fingers Rib House on the Greenville town square. Daniel was curious about the sauce rack, which contained Carolina sweet sauce, Tennessee whiskey sauce, and habanero sweet sauce, among others. I started to explain regional nuances in southern barbecue, but Daniel interrupted me.

"It all tastes the same," he sniffed.

"Dude, that's sacrilegious," I replied indignantly.

I stopped a server and said, "Ma'am, when you get a chance, I'd like to see the manager, please."

The manager, Cristina Creed, arrived quickly and assumed a defensive posture, arms crossed and grim, anticipating a complaint. The din from nearby tables quieted to a murmur as customers eavesdropped.

"Ma'am, this young man needs an attitude adjustment," I said.

Creed's eyebrow lifted as I repeated Daniel's heresy. Daniel fidgeted under Creed's smoldering glare and nervously burrowed into the booth's padded backrest. With professorial authority, Creed explained the differences between North Carolina, South Carolina and Georgia barbecue. Of course, those are entirely different from Memphis and Texas "Q" in terms of sauces and preparation. There are also wet and dry barbecues.

The only way to fully appreciate the subtleties, Creed continued, was with a taste test. She sent us a free sampler that contained nearly every item on the menu. We ate it all and nearly foundered. We walked many laps around the square to fend off a calorie-induced coma.

Our travels together forged a bond characterized by an uncommon depth of mutual respect and understanding. A young man learns a lot about his dad watching him work, and time on the road shows close companions what makes each other tick. Daniel and I were closest when hunting or fishing, and the value of our 2004 spring turkey hunt appreciates at an annual rate that would make the most successful hedge fund manager envious.

A cardinal rule when hunting with a newcomer, especially a child, is to downplay expectations. A born hyperbolist, I am not good at this. To hear me tell it, every hunt is bound to be epic. I all but guaranteed a gobbler to strut on the end of Daniel's shotgun barrel. All of my uptalk whipped Daniel into a low simmer on the morning of his first turkey hunt, and he was certain that success was ordained.

Naturally, turkeys vacated the farm that morning. We did not turn a gobble, and we saw no fresh sign. I called aggressively, and

I called quietly. I yelped and cutt without eliciting a peep of feedback. On a fabulous April morning in the heyday of Missouri's great turkey hunting boom, our prime spot had inexplicably gone barren.

It was hot and dusty when we returned to the truck at about 9 a.m. We cracked open cold sodas and assembled sandwiches of roast beef, ham, turkey, and cheese. I adorned mine with mustard, Miracle Whip, pickle, and onion. Dan's sandwich was plain save for a dab of mustard. He munched a kosher dill pickle on the side.

Legal hunting time for spring turkey season ends at 1 p.m. in Missouri, but Daniel was indifferent about continuing.

"We've got three more hours," I said. "You ready to get back after them?"

"I don't care," Daniel muttered.

"It's your hunt, Bud," I said. "We can try to make a play, or we can leave. I'm sure there's plenty for you to do at home."

Daniel understood the euphemism for schoolwork and chores.

"I want to hunt," he said hollowly.

"Turkeys are loafing and scratching in the woods right now," I said. "They'll get active again around eleven. Let's take a little power nap and regroup in thirty minutes or so."

The nap rejuvenated us, but we were still disheartened from the inactivity of the morning. If nothing else, maybe a change of scenery would improve our moods.

"Let's hunt the lower part of the farm around the creek bottom," I said. "Sometimes I see turkeys down there in the afternoon."

The creek cuts a fairly straight course through a narrow hollow between two gently sloping ridges. The farmhouse and outbuildings are on one side of the ridge. The opposite slope climaxes at Jake Ridge, which is heavily wooded. That slope contains a series of steep, narrow pastures that are perpendicular to the creek. Narrow fingers of thick cedar separate the pastures. A narrow pasture follows the creek. It gradually becomes overgrown before ending in a low cedar thicket.

Dan and I trudged along a cow trail below the farmhouse toward the edge where the creek bottom pasture yields to woods. I glanced to the left and saw a mob of dark shapes on the opposite slope.

"Turkeys!" I gasped as I grasped Daniel's shoulder. "There must be fifteen, twenty of them. There are probably more in the woods that we can't see!"

Though the distance between us was not far, our presence did not bother the turkeys, probably because they are accustomed to seeing people near the house. They strung parallel to the creek and headed to the end of the pasture toward the woods.

"Those birds are moving faster than you think, but if we can get ahead of them, we might be able to cut them off," I said. "Don't even look that way. Let's just scoot out of here real quick like they're not even there."

We ambled along until we entered a wooded area behind the farmhouse where we could no longer see the turkeys.

"Let's boogie across this creek and get into those woods," I said. "We can set up on that slope, and they'll come right to us."

We dashed down the hill and crossed the creek at a low ford, and then we splashed across wet gravel and scrambled up the dirt bank into the broken cover. We ducked behind a low rise that shielded us from sharp turkey eyes, and we waited. For nearly twenty minutes we saw only songbirds flitting among low branches. The urgency had ebbed.

"Looks like they gave us the slip," I said. "I'll bet when they got to the end of that field, they turned and went up the hill into one of those finger pastures. Maybe if we can get behind them and see where they're going, we might be able to loop around and get above them."

We stood and stretched before starting through the brush toward the pasture edge. We went about ten steps when I saw several mottled silhouettes in the brush ahead.

"Get down!" I hissed. "They're coming right to us!"

Daniel and I dropped prone under a shallow rise beneath a scrub cedar and tried to melt into the soil. We didn't even have time to mask our faces. We pressed to the ground and peered under our cap bills at the turkeys gathering before us. They massed at the edge of the brush line about twenty yards away, their number growing by twos and threes. Jakes comprised the vanguard, but hens clucked and cutt behind them, chasing and pecking their underlings.

"The gobblers are somewhere behind the hens," I whispered. "Every one of those birds is in range right now. Look for beards and shoot the biggest one you see. You know where to aim?"

"Right under the head," replied Daniel.

"Make it count!" I whispered.

The flock inched toward us and split into two groups to pass the tangle of cedar where Dan and I lay. Turkeys soon flanked us, with more following, but we had yet to see a mature gobbler.

"Too many hens," I whispered. "They'll bust us before the gobblers get here."

Finally, a jake spied us and came to investigate. At a distance of about five feet, it tilted its head and trained one eye upon us as if focusing a microscope on a petri dish. We feigned invisibility like two junior high scamps caught cheating on a test. After a moment of indecision, the jake retreated, "putt-putting" with increasing tempo and volume. Every other turkey stood erect and alert.

"We're busted!" I whispered. "Kill that jake!"

The last word was still in the air when my Super X2 thundered. The jake rolled into a flapping, flopping heap. Turkeys flew in every direction with the roar of a helicopter as feathers rained from the branches. Two turkeys nearly trampled our backs. Within seconds, we were alone except for Daniel's convulsing jake.

"Jayzus lawd a'mighty!" I giggled with a loud sigh.

Daniel rolled onto his side and laughed from his marrow at the cartoonish mayhem.

In one outing, Daniel accomplished what it took me years to do. He overcame a dismal first half and a dispirited halftime. He exploited unexpected opportunities with a bold move in the third quarter. He survived a near implosion from a premature move and then capitalized on a sudden stroke of good luck in the fourth quarter to claim an upset victory.

The jake was too heavy for Daniel to carry, but he strode beside me like a conquistador as I toted his bird back to the truck.

I hoped that experience would begin a lifelong partnership, one that should have accelerated when I became outdoors editor of the *Arkansas Democrat-Gazette* in 2005, but Daniel didn't hunt turkeys again. As much as he loved the outdoors, he didn't dwell on one square for long. He checked big events off his life card and quickly moved on to the next thing. He quit deer hunting in 2009 after killing his only deer as well. He stuck with duck hunting a little longer, but he was unwilling to tolerate the cold and sleep deprivation inherent to that sport.

Dan's duck hunting career started ideally when a friend invited us to an exclusive duck hunt at Hamptons Reservoir, a legendary duck hunting property near Stuttgart, Arkansas.

On the way to that hunt, at about 4:30 a.m., blue lights flashed behind me on the east side of England, Arkansas. An England police officer appeared at my window while his partner stood toward the rear of the vehicle.

"Sir, would you please step out of the vehicle?" asked the officer at the window. He directed me to the front of my truck where the second officer joined him.

"I just wanted to show you that you have a headlight out," he said.

"The hell!" I grunted. With catlike quickness, I smashed the side of my fist into the fender right behind the dysfunctional headlight. The light came on, like in *Happy Days* when The Fonz smacked the jukebox to play a record at Arnold's Drive-In. The officers glanced at each other with bewildered amusement, nonplussed at having been cheated out of writing a ticket.

"You've done this before," said the lead officer, sincerely impressed.

"Heyyy," I growled, spreading my arms and channeling The Fonz.

Both officers laughed.

"You going duck hunting?" asked the lead officer.

"Yes, sir. Me and my boy," I answered.

"Go on. Get out of here!" he said. "Have a safe hunt."

As always at Hamptons, ducks were as thick as mosquitoes that morning, and Daniel rapidly bagged a limit of six ducks with his 20-gauge pump-action shotgun. The voluminous shooting suited his personality. He was so excited that he declared himself a duck hunting disciple. On the way home, I stopped at a sporting goods store in Stuttgart and dropped a few hundred dollars to get him a proper pair of waders and parka.

Two weeks later, we celebrated Daniel's seventeenth birthday by skipping school and hunting ducks with our friend Alan Thomas at Lake Dardanelle near Clarksville, Arkansas. A fierce northeast wind made our eyes and noses run and immediately froze the discharge into a crusty veneer across our faces. It was a wet kind of cold that no amount of clothing deters, and our shivering made us sore. The coves splintering off the main lake were iced, as were the shallow tule fringes around the islands. Ducks were scarce. The three of us killed only two mallards and a Canada goose. Daniel was miserable.

"You've had it as good as it gets, and today you had it as bad as it gets," I said. "Now you can call yourself a duck hunter."

That was Daniel's last hunt of any kind.

He actually began drifting away the night I called a team meeting with my three sons to tell them I had cancer.

"I need you guys to carry some of my weight," I said. "I'm not going to be worth a damn around here for the next few months, and your mother is going to need all of you to take up the slack. I need you to look after your sisters and do whatever needs done to keep this place running."

My youngest son, Matthew, then thirteen, curled into a ball in my arms and bawled. Ethan, a freshman on full academic scholarship at Henderson State University in Arkadelphia, Arkansas, offered to quit school and get a job to help support the family. Daniel stood at the foot of the bed, hand over his mouth, eyes dark and glassy with fear and confusion. He had always regarded me as a superman, and something as insignificant as a piddling, no-account little cancer was going to take down his hero.

Something snapped inside him that night. The changes were subtle at first, but they became more pronounced with time. He disengaged from school and school sports. He departed from his ethics and moral principles. He lost his drive and rejected his pursuit of excellence. Alcohol and drugs, opioids in particular, filled the void. He took up petty larceny to pay for his habits, and then he began dealing.

Daniel stayed true to one dream, though. From early adolescence, his unshakeable goal was to serve in the United States Marine

Corps. His mother and I implored him to go to college and enter through the Reserve Officers' Training Corps, but Daniel wanted no more school. He insisted on doing it the way he did everything: the hard way. The wars in Iraq and Afghanistan still raged, but I accepted the possibility that the Marines might be Daniel's best opportunity to regain his moorings.

Years before, my wife had a dream in which she said God told her that Daniel would leave us and go far away. I accepted the possibility that her dream was prophetic and that military service would take him to the far reaches of the world for an extended time. He would come back. Daniel always came back. Hopefully, he would come back a better man. Daniel was determined to enlist. He was an adult. I couldn't stop him, so I gave him my blessing.

Immediately after graduating from high school in 2012, Daniel entered basic training at San Diego. After graduating from boot camp, he returned home for a short leave before resuming his training at Camp Pendleton. While home, he attended a party where he smoked marijuana and took hydrocodone.

Reporting back for duty, Daniel failed a drug screen. The Marine Corps discharged him under "other than honorable conditions." While Daniel awaited discharge, the Marines made an example of him. He was held in virtual isolation and was forbidden to interact with other Marines except for a few others in a similar predicament. The Corps boasts that it never leaves one of its own on a battlefield, but it abandoned Daniel. The Corps trained him to be a remorseless instrument of war, fermented him in a sour mash of resentment and victimhood, and then unleashed him on the world without rehabilitation or deprogramming.

Defeated, humiliated, and stripped of his self-image, Daniel returned home and yielded entirely to his vices and enablers. He embraced the rural drug culture and began dealing contraband on a larger scale to augment income from a steady stream of menial jobs. When he involved a younger sibling in his misdeeds, I forbade them all from interacting with him unsupervised.

Moral barriers obliterated, Daniel became increasingly violent and cruel. He boasted about having participated in home invasions with a posse of brigands in Colorado and Utah, the same Marines who were drummed out for drug offenses at the same time as Daniel. In Florida, his group assaulted homeless camps at night, beating inhabitants. Of one such raid, Daniel bragged of pushing a shopping cart full of the homeless people's possessions in front of an oncoming train.

In 2015, I played my last card. I texted Daniel and told him to accompany me to an Arkansas Game and Fish Commission work meeting I was covering.

"I have a class at eleven," he replied.

"The most interesting part will be before then," I said. "You don't have to stay long. I think you'd enjoy seeing how public policy gets crafted behind the scenes."

Daniel was a gym rat with a body of sculpted marble, thanks also in part to aggressive steroid use that doubtless affected his personality. Despite his habits, he dressed sharply and groomed himself immaculately, and he retained a stolid military bearing. He sat with me for about thirty minutes before quietly exiting to attend his class at the University of Arkansas at Little Rock.

The Game and Fish Commission held its monthly public meeting the next morning. When the crowd thinned after the meeting's conclusion, Game and Fish Commission Director Mike Knoedl and his chief of staff Jeff Crow bracketed me at the media table. Before becoming director, Knoedl had served as chief of law enforcement for the commission, as had Crow. Both had served long careers as

Arkansas game wardens. Crow had also served with the Arkansas State Police and was a captain in the U.S. Marine Corps reserve.

"Was that your boy at the committee meetings yesterday?" Knoedl asked.

"Yeah, that was Daniel," I said. "He was curious about what goes on at these meetings. I think for some class on public policy that he's taking. I hope he wasn't in the way."

"I thought that's who it was," Knoedl said. "He looks just like you."

"Ha! Maybe in my dreams I looked like that, a long, long time ago!" I said with a laugh.

"He's studying over there at UALR?" Knoedl asked. "What's he majoring in?"

"Criminal justice, I think," I said. "It's hard to pin him down sometimes."

Knoedl and Crow exchanged a look.

"I don't want to get in your business, but Col. Crow and I have been talking, and we were wondering if your boy might consider a career as a wildlife officer," Knoedl said.

"I don't know if he's thought that far ahead, but I'll ask him," I said.

Daniel dismissed the idea immediately.

"Game wardens don't make any money," he scoffed.

"How much are you making now?" I asked.

Daniel glowered.

"It's a hell of an opportunity," I pressed. "The lifestyle suits you perfectly. You'll spend most of your time outdoors, and game wardens have an esprit de corps very much like the Marines. They've got that 'family thing' that appeals to you. I think you'd find with them the same things that attracted you to the Corps."

Daniel sulked, refusing to meet my eyes.

"They also have a really cool uniform," I added, grasping for anything that might pierce his defenses.

"They do have some sweet unis," Daniel acknowledged grudgingly.

"Hear them out, Daniel," I implored. "It could be the best thing that ever happened to you."

Daniel was stoned senseless for a private interview with Knoedl and Crow. They were appalled. Daniel blew his last best opportunity, and his downward spiral accelerated. Every night I went to bed dreading the phone call that would confirm my deepest fears. Sometimes I woke in the middle of the night and immediately went to my knees to pray him out of some precarious situation that I sensed in my sleep. Such was our bond, and I begged daily for God to release Daniel from the shackles of his addictions.

May 28, 2016, was an uncommonly beautiful morning in Hot Spring County, Arkansas. It was a Saturday, the beginning of the Memorial Day weekend. Every window in the house was opened to let in the warm breeze. Bluebirds tended to a clutch of nestlings in a house beside the driveway that my daughter made for Father's Day the year before.

Hearing the soft crunch of rubber on gravel, I peeked out the bathroom window curtain. Two Arkansas State Police cruisers crept into the driveway like cats stalking prey.

I greeted the two troopers at the door, invited them inside, and offered them coffee. They politely declined. This was not a social visit.

Trooper Brian Burke removed his hat and asked, "Does a Daniel Philip Hendricks live here?"

"Not currently," I replied. "He's, uh, living with his girlfriend somewhere in Saline County."

"May I ask your name, sir?" Burke asked.

"My name is Bryan Hendricks."

"Are you related to Daniel?" Burke asked.

"I am," I replied warily.

"May I ask your relationship to the young man?" Burke asked. His tone was increasingly somber.

"I'm his father." I replied.

"Can you confirm Daniel's birthday?" Burke asked.

"Yes sir. He was born Jan. 17, 1994," I replied. "Officer, is my son in some kind of trouble?"

Burke glanced at his partner and then looked back at me.

"Sir," Burke said softly, "Daniel was involved in an accident on Highway 70 near the Garland County line at about seven o'clock this morning."

Burke hesitated and looked at the floor.

"And?" I asked.

Burke rubbed his thumbs across the brim of his hat and then lifted his eyes to meet mine. "Mr. Hendricks, your son did not survive the accident."

At age 22, Tiger Dan was finally free. Not in the way I hoped, but compassion is not always gentle.

CHAPTER EIGHT

THE WITNESS

An enduring mystery to readers of my columns in the *Arkansas Democrat-Gazette* from 2007–11 was the identity of a recurring character known as "The Witness."

He first appeared in July 2007 in a column about a mature tom that persistently gobbled in the heat of a summer day at a hunting camp in southeast Arkansas. Turkeys rarely gobble that late in the year, and I mentioned it only because I had a witness.

We hunted many times together in the quixotic pursuit of an elusive black squirrel, producing a series of articles that spanned about two years. Nodding to the July gobbler incident, I always identified my partner as The Witness, and there was considerable speculation about who it was.

His name is Sheffield Nelson, a prominent Arkansas attorney, philanthropist, and political figure. In an era when the Democratic Party monopolized Arkansas politics, Nelson helped reestablish the presence and later the prominence of the Republican Party. He lost to Bill Clinton in the 1990 Arkansas gubernatorial election, setting up Clinton's successful campaign for the presidency in 1992.

A charismatic, larger-than-life character, Nelson is a fanatical hunter whose personality afield is far different than his public persona. He took former Governor Mike Huckabee on some of Huckabee's first deer hunts, including one where Huckabee killed a large-racked buck that Nelson strapped to the roof of his black Chevy Suburban for the trip back to Little Rock. Driving to the Governor's Mansion, Nelson and Huckabee made a detour down President Clinton Avenue, in the heart of Little Rock's trendy and bustling River Market District. Huckabee, a master of public relations who carefully guarded a jocular but dignified public image, waved to the throngs milling in front of the bars and bistros to a chorus of cheers, jeers, and blaring car horns.

Word gets around fast in a town as small as Little Rock. When the pair arrived at the Governor's Mansion a few blocks away, Sheffield's wife, Mary Lynn Nelson, waited at the gate. Jabbing her finger against Huckabee's chest, the voice of reason in the Nelson family insisted that Huckabee conduct himself in a manner more befitting his position.

"And YOU!" Mary Lynn unleashed a fusillade at her delightedly unrepentant husband.

Nelson did the same thing with two deer that we killed while hunting together in the Ozark Mountains of Madison County. He parked the Suburban in front of a restaurant and got a table near the window to assess the reaction. Some diners took cell phone photos in front of the deer. Others grumbled. Nelson, his antenna always tuned to polls, duly noted that favorable reactions outnumbered unfavorable by about three to one.

As a member of the Arkansas Game and Fish Commission from 2000–07, Nelson befriended me in 2005 when I became the outdoors editor of the *Arkansas Democrat-Gazette*. Nelson recognized that only one media member covers the Game and Fish Commission. Whether a commissioner likes that reporter or not, it behooves the agency to empower that reporter to be a reliable, accurate, and unassailable conduit to the public.

Our relationship was complex. Nelson was a surprisingly bountiful and candid source, but we communicated professionally, with businesslike detachment. He taught me how to interpret the internal vernacular within the commission and its administrative staff, enabling me to filter static and cut to the heart of the issues they confronted.

Why does that matter? Next to the state highway commission, the Arkansas Game and Fish Commission is the state's most powerful and most influential agency. Authorized in 1944 by Amendment 35 to the Arkansas Constitution, it is independent from the state's legislative and executive branches. The governor appoints the seven commission members but has little influence on them thereafter. The legislature has even less influence because of Amendment 35's mandatory political separation.

In addition to income from hunting and fishing licenses, Amendment 75—enacted in 1997—provides the Game and Fish Commission a dedicated source of funding with a statewide, ⅛-percent conservation sales tax. The commission shares the tax revenue with three other state agencies. The Game and Fish Commission's portion of Amendment 75 revenues is forty-five percent.

Additionally, the commission receives revenue from federal excise taxes authorized by the Pittman-Robertson and Dingell-Johnson Acts. Untouchable and independently funded, the Game and Fish Commission is a de facto fourth branch of Arkansas government. It touches the lives of nearly every Arkansan as well as thousands of hunters and anglers that visit from outside the state.

According to the "2011 National Survey of Fishing, Hunting and Wildlife-Associated Recreation," compiled by the U.S. Fish and Wildlife Service and U.S. Census Bureau, hunting, fishing, and other wildlife-related recreation generate about $1.8 billion in economic activity annually in Arkansas and support thousands of jobs. Because of the agency's reach and mystique, an appointment to the Game and Fish Commission, though unpaid, is one of the most coveted seats in Arkansas state government.

Nelson gave me an advanced perspective on the agency as well as insight into its intricate inner workings and internal politics. Through him, I came to understand the delicate relationships between the commission and the legislature, the commission and the governor, and the commission and the agency's staff as well as the internal politics among the agency's staff independent of the commissioners.

It is a fascinating study in human dynamics to observe seven wealthy, alpha males (the first female was appointed to a full term in 2019) all jockeying for position and influence in a small group setting. No matter how big a fish somebody is, there is almost always a bigger fish. For some, it is a rude realization. Others navigate the turbulent waters masterfully. Coupled with the unscripted things that unpolished, amateur political figures do and say, the drama makes the Game and Fish Commission the liveliest, most colorful, and most unpredictable beat in Arkansas journalism.

It is risky for a journalist to get close to a person he covers, but Nelson was media savvy and respected our boundaries. The late Bill Simmons, the *Democrat-Gazette's* august political editor, once demanded to know the identity of The Witness. He was not amused when I quipped that I never reveal my sources, so I acquiesced and divulged Nelson's name.

"What's the point of calling him The Witness?" Simmons asked sharply.

"Because these aren't news stories," I replied. "They're entertainment. A couple of guys out chasing squirrels. Not trophy bucks or green timber mallards at some blue-blood hunting club, but squirrels! My readers are billionaires, food stamp recipients, and everyone in between. The Witness is somebody they can all relate to. Injecting Sheffield's name into it changes the whole tone, and it would make me look like a braggart. That would defeat the purpose."

"What does Sheffield think about that?" Simmons asked, voice softening.

"It relieves him from the burden of being Sheffield the public figure," I answered. "He enjoys it because it allows him to be himself. A lot of people suspect it's him anyway from clues in the articles. People ask him about it all the time. He gets a big kick out of that, but he never admits to it."

Simmons smiled wryly and nodded.

Several important hard news stories fell on my shoulders during Nelson's tenure. One came to my attention in 2006 by way of an anonymous note in a manila envelope that somebody deposited at the *Democrat-Gazette's* front desk. Two Arkansas Game and Fish Commission game wardens were cited in Mississippi for hunting turkeys without having bought Mississippi hunting licenses. One was the assistant chief of the Game and Fish Commission's law enforcement division and heir apparent to the agency's top law enforcement position. The National Wild Turkey Federation had recently honored the other game warden as its Arkansas Wildlife Officer of the Year. The agency refused to release information about the incident or even acknowledge the incident occurred on the basis that it was a personnel matter and thus exempt from disclosure under the state's Freedom of Information Act (FOIA).

Nelson was torn over the public relations dilemma the incident created for the agency, and I was frustrated at the agency using FOIA to suppress a major news story.

"Rumors are already out there on the internet, but rumors are always worse than the real story," I said. "This thing is taking on a life of its own and getting more and more outrageous the longer it lives. And because Game and Fish thinks it can play possum until it blows over, the agency just has to sit there and roast in a fire of its own making."

Nelson nodded slowly, pinching the corners of his mouth with his thumb and forefinger.

"Here's what else is going to happen," I said. "I guarantee you that every outlaw that gets cited for a turkey hunting violation is going to shove this deal in an officer's face: 'If Game and Fish employees can poach, then, by God, so can I!' Every single officer in this agency will be guilty by association. It'll blow their credibility all to hell."

"I know it," Nelson said. "I've been thinking the exact same thing."

"There's a graceful way to resolve it," I offered. "The *Democrat-Gazette* is the journal of record for this state, and only we are in the position to report the facts without sensationalizing them. I can do one big story, lay it all out there, and be done with it. If Game and Fish demonstrates that it's held those officers accountable, I think the public will be satisfied, and it will put all the conjecture and conspiracy stuff to rest within a week."

"Those guys have put a cloud over the rest of our employees and even us as commissioners. I hate it," Nelson said. "This is exactly the kind of thing that destroys morale within the agency and erodes trust with the public."

Nelson was silent for a long while as he contemplated the delicate balance between public transparency and a commissioner's loyalty to the agency's employees. In the end, Nelson concluded that all of the agency's employees shouldn't suffer for the misdeeds of a few. In this context, transparency equated to loyalty.

"I think one big story is exactly the right way to handle it," Nelson finally said. "Better to take our medicine and turn the page."

The next morning, the Game and Fish Commission released the documents, which produced a front-page story the following morning. Among the details was the assistant chief's demotion to a dead-end position running the agency's youth shooting sports program. He languished there for several years before finally leaving the agency. The documents also noted that the other officer was demoted in rank and pay; his prospects for advancement effectively suspended.

After Nelson's term on the commission expired and there was no conflict of interest, we hunted together as friends. We shared a passion for turkey hunting, and we pursued turkeys zealously at a place called Jackson Point. It is one of many oxbow islands in the Mississippi River that are isolated from the mainland inside the giant levees that hold back the great river during floods. The game-rich islands are privately owned. Many are cooperatives, and single memberships cost six figures. Each member at Jackson Point has a personal lodge. One, a prominent Little Rock banker, even has a personal airstrip on the island with a Chevy Suburban parked permanently so he can drive to and from his lodge.

It was here that Nelson and Mike Huckabee triggered a minor security crisis. Cell service is available only among the lodges at the high-ground center of the island. Nelson and Huckabee went deer hunting on a remote part of the island where their all-terrain vehicle ran out of fuel, forcing them to walk several miles back to camp in the dark. Unable to contact the governor and not knowing even his approximate whereabouts, Huckabee's security detail panicked.

Minutes away from issuing a dreaded "The governor is missing," alert, Huckabee's security staff was profoundly relieved when the pair trudged into camp late in the evening.

Because of the Mississippi River's meanderings, some islands on Mississippi's side of the river are in Arkansas's jurisdiction and some islands on Arkansas's side of the river are in Mississippi's jurisdiction. Some, like Jackson Point, contain land in both states. Will Primos's legendary Cottonmouth, where so many Primos videos were shot, lies within Arkansas, Mississippi, and Louisiana. If you hunt or fish on Mississippi's portion of the island, you are subject to Mississippi's game and fish regulations, and so on.

Clubs like Jackson Point are managed primarily for trophy white-tailed deer, but they also support the largest turkey populations in the Mississippi River Delta. Fewer hunters pursue turkeys than deer, so pressure on turkeys is relatively light.

The landscape is flat and defined by deep, sandy loam that the Mississippi River deposited over millennia. The bottomland forests are young and contain bitter pecan, various berry-producing hardwoods, and dense, brushy thickets. Lacing the entire island is a vast network of food plots planted in clover, rye, wheat, chufa, chicory, peas, and other high-quality wildlife foods. Here, in Nelson's company, I killed my first mature gobbler in Arkansas during the 2008 spring turkey season. I killed another gobbler at his side on the Mississippi side of the island.

To reduce noise, Nelson scouts by driving the interior roads in a battery-powered all-terrain vehicle. He uses decoys for turkey hunting, but his decoys are much fancier than the retail plastic variety. They are taxidermic mounts of hen turkeys that he killed in Missouri while hunting in the fall with his friend and fellow Arkansan Jerry Jones, owner of the Dallas Cowboys. Before each season, Nelson sends his "girls" to a taxidermist to repair damage inflicted by live turkeys.

In the spring of 2009, I was treated for rectal cancer. Initially, I underwent five weeks of radiation therapy and an extended period of chemotherapy. The treatments reduced me to a physical and emotional shell, but Nelson insisted that turkey hunting was the right prescription for recovery. He was prescient. I was astonished at how a few days in Jackson Point's turkey woods gave me respite from pain, nausea, and malaise. My treatment ended in November 2009, but it took two years for me to regain my strength. Nelson, of course, insisted that turkey hunting remain an integral element in my recovery.

Early in the journey, I was strong enough to hunt in the mornings, but fatigue put me down for long naps in the afternoon. We resumed hunting at about 2 p.m. On one particular morning in April 2011, I felt unusually resilient. We hunted in the morning, broke for brunch, and resumed hunting at about 11 a.m. Nelson wanted to hunt a spot that was too confined to accommodate a partner, so he directed me to a small field planted with oats and winter wheat. Thick woods surrounded the field, which was accessible by a tractor road.

The spot was ideal. I sat against a big hackberry tree that shielded me from behind. The thicket's curvature also concealed me from the sides. A thin beard of brush between the food plot and me fragmented my silhouette from the front. I placed a plastic decoy about twenty yards in front at an angle so that an approaching gobbler would be less likely to look my direction.

Mosquitoes swarmed as soon as I sat. I ignited my Thermacell, a device that emits insect-repelling vapors, and it vanquished the mosquitoes within minutes. Their absence made for a positively dreamy atmosphere. It was sunny and warm, with a hint of breeze that rustled the leaves above. Songbirds flitted in the brush. Robins bounced among the furrows while blue jays taunted and heckled from above.

With a box call, slate, and diaphragm, I performed my usual alternating routine. As was my habit in those days, I called too much and too loud, but on this occasion I attracted an audience.

A gobble boomed from the road leading to the food plot. The tom gobbled several more times in response to my calls, and after a few minutes he marched into the food plot with a subordinate gobbler in tow. High-stepping across the furrows, he presented himself to the decoy and unfurled his royal robe.

Nineteen times out of twenty, that would have been a tagged gobbler. Unfortunately, this time was number twenty. Beginning in the 2011 season, the Arkansas Game and Fish Commission enacted a regulation that made it illegal for adult hunters to kill immature gobblers. The agency passed the no-jakes regulation in response to a precipitously declining turkey population. At its core, the regulation intended to reduce the gobbler harvest, which it accomplished, but protecting juvenile males also allows more toms to survive to prime breeding age. The no-jakes rule was very controversial at the time, but it certainly didn't hurt. From anecdotal evidence, I believe it helped, but it tested my resolve on that occasion.

In Arkansas, a legal gobbler must have a beard longer than six inches or a fan containing uniform length feathers, without the telltale "finger" feathers in the middle of a jake's fan that rise above the others. This gobbler had a tiny little beard that pointed straight out like a pencil, and it looked shorter than six inches.

For about forty minutes, the tom put on a show that would have shamed Freddie Mercury. He gobbled and strutted while his subordinate hovered in the background, but the strutter never gave me a direct view of his fan. He only gave me side views, but he retracted his fan when he faced me or turned away.

Multiple times the gobbler turned to leave, and multiple times I called him back, but I could not determine his legality. I could have rationalized that a tom gobbling so forcefully in the company of a subordinate tom was certainly two years old, but I would not take that chance. If I shot the bird and it was legal, I would merely have gambled and won. A cardinal rule of hunting is to always be certain of your target. As the bird folded his feathers and headed for the woods, I lowered my gun and watched him walk away.

Nelson anguished as I recapped the encounter over lunch.

"Gosh dang it, you'd think a bird that gobbles has got to be mature, especially if he's got a buddy like that one did," Nelson said.

"He had to be, but that stubby little beard was all I had to go on," I lamented. "You're awfully generous to have me down here, and I would hate to do anything that would cause you to regret it."

"Well, then, we'll just find you another one," Nelson declared.

After lunch, Nelson and I entered a long section of woods not far from the morning food plot that leads to another field. A hillside plunges into a shallow ravine, rises up the other side, and continues to a nearby slough. I ignited my Thermacell, sat against a tree on the hillside, and I called.

Within about thirty minutes, three gobblers appeared in the thicket and strolled across the knoll. They ignored the calls, but the biggest gobbler walked in front of my gun at a distance of about forty yards. I rolled the bird, but it bounced up and sprinted toward the slough where it would probably crawl into a bramble and die or be eaten by scavengers in the night. I jumped up and lumbered after the stricken gobbler, oblivious to the deadfalls, snags, and armadillo burrows that could have sent me sprawling or broken a leg. I gained on the wounded turkey and killed it as it vaulted over a log. It weighed about twenty-two pounds, and its beard was almost twelve inches long.

I don't know who was happier, Nelson or me. I was gratified to know that I was, in my depleted state, still swift enough to run down a wounded turkey. I also believed the gobbler was a cosmic reward for my restraint earlier in the day. Most welcome was the rush of vibrancy that surged through my soul. I hadn't felt that good in a long time. It was like moonlight in the midnight of my life.

The Witness noticed it, too, and he prescribed more of it.

CHAPTER NINE

WOODSTOCK

The name Woodstock is sacred among music lovers, but in Arkansas, it is also revered among the state's hunting elite.

Woodstock Island, like Jackson Point, is an oxbow island in the Mississippi River near Lake Village, Arkansas. Like other Mississippi River islands, Woodstock's owners manage it primarily for trophy white-tailed deer, but its diverse habitat also supports large numbers of Eastern wild turkeys. Freddie Black, a bank executive and former member of the Arkansas Game and Fish Commission, said that Woodstock Island supplied a large number of turkeys for relocation when the commission reintroduced turkeys across Arkansas in the mid-1900s.

In 2008, Black invited me to hunt with him and Nelson at Woodstock. Buoyed from recent success, I fancied myself worthy of such an honor, but Woodstock would humble me.

My guide for the visit was Greg Hillis, who is known as one of the best turkey hunters in southeast Arkansas. A delicate dance occurs when a hunter and guide meet for the first time as the pair appraises each other's measure. The first step in the dance is a conversation about hunting. It is a one-sided interview to determine the client's capabilities and to determine whether the hunt will

92

be a partnership or a babysitting exercise. Experienced guides are adept at sifting wheat from chaff, but occasionally a weed slips through the screen. Like a high-school athlete shopping his talents to prospective colleges, I only included highlights in my reel, and Hillis bought the act.

After a short lunch, Hillis and I descended into the island's interior for an afternoon hunt. As we walked the edge of a freshly plowed field, Hillis saw dark shapes at the edge of a distant tree line. With his binoculars, he identified at least one mature gobbler in a group of hens and jakes.

"It's going to be hard to close on them in the open like this," I said.

"Won't need to close on them," Hillis said assertively. "That gobbler will come to us."

The turkeys were about 400 yards away, but Hillis yelped and cackled on his diaphragm call. I was astonished that a turkey could hear it at that distance. I was even more surprised when the gobbler hesitated while the rest of his flock continued.

"It's on!" Hillis said. "Come with me!"

We ducked into the woods abutting the field and sat against trees at the edge of a tractor road. Hillis continued calling. I wasn't surprised that the bird gobbled, but I was very surprised that he gobbled so close. He had covered a lot of ground quickly.

"Get your gun up," Hillis instructed, drawing a wide triangle through the woods with his finger. "He might hang up, or he might come running in."

The margin of error was slim. The woods were open and level, enabling a turkey to see us long before he was in range. With a stable backrest and a highly competent caller to close the deal, I was comfortable and confident.

A flash of buff and brown flickered in the brush. It was a strutting gobbler. He zig-zagged closer and closer until he appeared in an opening, dappled light flashing across his outstretched fan. The gobbler was hot and committed, so there was no hurry. He was coming.

The bird stepped out of the brush and into a clearing. I sensed he was in range, and all of the circuits in my internal fire control system flashed green. I fired, but it was too soon. The bird toppled but regained its footing.

"Get on him!" Hillis barked.

I fired again but missed as the turkey sprinted into the brush. We searched in widening circles out to about 200 yards, but we didn't find so much as a feather.

Hillis's demeanor changed. His good humor became stern. I had rushed a shot at a bird that clearly intended to come much closer. Hillis's glare declared that I was on probation.

We met again the next morning before dawn. Hillis had roosted a flock of turkeys that included a couple of big gobblers. If we all kept to the script, we would be done before breakfast. We chose a concealed setup as the toms gobbled on the roost. Soon, we heard them fly to the ground. Before long, a phalanx of hens approached with a mature, strutting gobbler in tow. My gun barrel bobbed and weaved as I struggled to attain a more comfortable shooting position.

"Quit moving!" Hillis hissed.

The gobbler must have seen me move because he flattened his plumage and hesitated. Again he was too far, but I fired anyway. This time there was no need to search. I missed cleanly, and the turkeys evacuated. It's one thing to miss a turkey in range. It's stupid to shoot at a bird out of range that you have already spooked.

Hillis had seen enough.

"Good luck," he said coolly. "I'm going hunting."

Hillis turned and walked away, leaving me standing alone.

I had a long morning to brood. I feared that word of my gaffes would spread quickly among my friends at camp. I had disgraced myself in front of an accomplished and honorable hunter. I had lost his respect, and these kinds of stories have a way of trickling onto the internet and its malicious message boards.

It reminded me of an episode of the *Andy Griffith Show*, when a young doctor moved to Mayberry. Andy invited the doctor to enjoy Thanksgiving dinner with the Taylor family, but they were horrified to learn that the doctor couldn't properly carve a turkey. Word spread quickly, and the good people of Mayberry construed that the doctor was incompetent. Like the physician and his roasted turkey, having missed two wild turkeys took a major bite out of my credibility. Worse, the wounds were all self-inflicted.

To salvage the day, I first needed to reestablish my priorities. My ego was bruised, but that represented a character deficiency that was far more egregious than my situational incompetence. Ego should never factor into hunting. If one hunts for self-aggrandizement, then one hunts for the wrong reason. Hunting should honor the game, not the hunter. No matter what the game, the game deserves the utmost respect. Killing game to stroke one's ego disrespects the game and all of its traditions. Hunting—and writing about hunting— to impress the public offends the ethics of hunting. Egoism has no place in any field of journalism, especially not in a field of journalism in which taking life is elemental to the beat.

"Get over yourself, and do it right," I cajoled myself. "The rest will take care of itself."

As the sting abated, I consoled myself by rationalizing that I simply had made a couple of boneheaded plays. I did nothing that was illegal or unethical. I might be a lousy turkey hunter, but I wasn't a slob turkey hunter. To quote Miles Davis, "It's not the note you play that's the wrong note. It's the note you play afterwards that makes it right or wrong."

At the risk of sounding trite, that moment changed my philosophy about hunting. Henceforth, I would call up my own gobblers. I would work every gobbler as close as possible, and I would stop trying only when it is clear that a bird will come no closer. My goal would be to call turkeys into my lap. I would not cut corners, and I would not do anything that I would be ashamed for anyone else to see. That became my turkey hunting mission statement.

I pocketed two other lessons from that experience. The gobbler I missed the previous day demonstrated the magic of a late afternoon turkey hunt. From that point forward, afternoon hunting became my specialty.

Second, I recognized how uncomfortable I am hunting with a guide. The caller alone bonds to the gobbler. The caller alone senses a gobbler's mood, and the caller alone recognizes the ebbs and flows of the seduction. It is an intimate relationship.

A designated shooter is merely a spectator, but he is also a subordinate. The guide picks the spot and sets the pace and the cadence. The shooter's instincts are irrelevant. When a gobbler comes in range, the need for quiet imposes a communications blackout at the most critical moment. It clouds my instincts because I am more tuned to the guide than I am to the turkey. A guide is a distraction. I cannot function with that amount of mental static. I must pilot my own ship.

My missteps with Hillis ensured that I would be alone for the rest of this hunt, and that was fine with me. I returned to the lodge and was relieved to find that the rest of the group was still afield.

That meant I wouldn't have to answer any questions or share any details of the morning's events. I wolfed down a sandwich and set out solo for the afternoon.

Another bit of mental static that clouded my subconscious was doubt about my shotgun's pattern. The gun was a Winchester Super X2 that had served me well to this point, but missing the previous day's gobbler unnerved me. I believed that the turkey had been in range, but that my pattern was off center or splotchy. I would not shoot at another turkey until I resolved that question.

One might think that the camp at Woodstock would have a proper patterning board, but no. The principal visitors to Woodstock use turkey guns that are professionally tuned with lengthened forcing cones and fitted with custom-made choke tubes and electronic optics. Their guns are factory patterned to a specific load. They use these guns only for turkeys, and they don't ever change components.

At that time, I used a stock shotgun with a regular bead sight and a factory Invector Plus full-choke tube. It had worked fine to that point, but I had to resolve my doubts. I walked to the bank of the Mississippi River, aimed at a spot on the water about twenty-five yards out, and fired. It was no substitute for a patterning board, but the pattern was tight and dense, concentrated at my aim point. The gun and load were fine within my comfortable parameters.

After a couple of hours scouting, I found an excellent place to sit at the base of a big tree that was down in a depression beside a tractor road. The low branches created a shadowy lair. The rise, with its tufts of tall, sparse grass, concealed my outline. The tree shielded me from behind. It was such a fine natural blind that I willed myself to kill a gobbler there.

With a slate call and diaphragm, I broadcast a bulletin. Within about fifteen minutes, a tom gobbled from a thicket on the other side of the road. Like a talk show host stepping from behind a curtain, a jake hopped into the clear. He turned to one side and gobbled. He turned to the other side and gobbled again. I slowly nestled the shotgun's butt pad into my shoulder and lined up the beads on the jake's neck. I ran down a quick mental checklist to ascertain that it was a legal gobbler, and then I squeezed the trigger.

The jake was a conspicuous downgrade in quality from the gobblers Hillis called up, but it was an honest reward for a reborn turkey hunter. It was also my last jake. From then on, I would hunt only mature gobblers.

It was a long walk back to the lodge through sandy, furrowed soil with a gobbler slung over my shoulder, but my steps were light. Halfway back to the lodge, Sheffield Nelson and our friend Sonny Varnell rolled up in an electric all-terrain vehicle. They were ecstatic about my jake and congratulated me heartily.

Back at the lodge, I placed the jake on the veranda. Upon returning from his hunt, Freddie Black saw the jake and asked who killed it.

"That's Bryan's bird," Nelson said, beaming. "He had a hell of a hunt!"

A smile spread across Black's face. He placed the unlit stub of his cigar upon the jake's body as a seal of approval.

Chapter Ten

THE MAGIC BARREL

I met Glenn Clark in 1994 when I was outdoors editor for the *Southwest Times-Record* in Fort Smith, Arkansas. Clark was a field representative for a fishing lure company. Our first outing together was a float fishing trip on the Caddo River in western Arkansas to shoot photos for a smallmouth bass fishing assignment for *Arkansas Sportsman* magazine.

It was Thanksgiving eve. The sky was leaden, damp, and cold. The river was deserted. An outfitter deposited Clark, me, and two canoes on a gravel bar at Glenwood. Only after the outfitter departed did Clark reveal that he had never paddled solo in a canoe.

"You mean to tell me you grew up in Oregon, and you've never paddled a canoe before?" I asked.

"I've paddled in a canoe lots of times," Clark said. "I've just never paddled one by myself."

"Well, that might be a bit of a problem because I've never been on this section of the river before," I said. "I don't know what we might run into down here as far as rapids, strainers, and stuff. Stay close, and let's take it easy. We should be okay."

Another problem paddling a river for the first time is that I didn't know any landmarks to gauge distance or location. It gets dark early in November, but heavy cloud cover further dimmed the pale light. We also started much later than was advisable for an eight-mile float through unfamiliar water. That's because we stopped to fish several creeks on the drive down, hoping to catch a couple of picture fish and render the canoe trip unnecessary.

We were already pinched for time, but every new stretch of water on the Caddo looked promising, and we fished hard for several hours without a bite. Finally, my inner alarm clock rang.

"What time is it?" I asked.

"Almost four," Clark replied.

"It'll be dark in two hours, and we've only gone about a mile and a half," I said. "We'd better kick it into gear."

That was about the time Clark casually mentioned that he and his wife were scheduled to leave for Nashville, Tennessee, that evening to spend Thanksgiving with her family. They needed to be on the road by 7 p.m., he said absently, as if talking to himself. Meeting that deadline was out of the question, but it was pointless to mention it.

We still had not gotten our photos, and the water looked too good not to fish, so we remained diligently on task. When the sun finally set around 6 p.m., it was as if someone had flipped off a light switch. It went black. There was no light from above, and since that portion of the river is wooded and undeveloped, there was no light from the banks either. Cell phones were still a novelty in 1994, so we also had no means to communicate with our outfitter or with our spouses.

When canoeing unfamiliar water in the dark, you must go slowly and with utmost caution. Since this part of the river is mostly long, deep pools separated by narrow, serpentine rapids, I deemed it safe to go well ahead of Clark and scout the bottlenecks. When

I heard rushing water, I got out of my canoe and walked it through the rapids.

In daylight, all the rapids were clear. As soon as the sun went down, fallen trees blocked every one of them.

"Glenn, there's a tree across this chute!" I shouted.

In the darkness I heard the slap and splash of hard paddle strokes.

"What's that about a tree?" Clark shouted.

His words echoing, Clark crashed into the tree, sending fishing tackle clattering amid a torrent of mutterings while Clark struggled to keep his canoe upright. It happened at least four times.

We reached our takeout at about 9 p.m. I officially quit smoking on New Year's Day 1985, but in those days I still cheated a little by carrying a pack of Swisher Sweets cigars in my tackle box. The smoke kept gnats and mosquitoes out of my face.

"How about that! I forgot all about these Swisher Sweets!" I exclaimed joyfully.

Clark, who was seething, suddenly got happy.

"You got cigars? I'll take one!" he said.

I handed Clark a cigar. He chomped on its plastic mouthpiece while I rummaged around in my tacklebox and then in my camera box.

"Aw, hell! I don't have a lighter," I said, dejected.

The remnants of Clark's goodwill fell to ashes. He scolded me as we pulled our canoes onto the boat ramp and organized our gear for pickup, which at that late hour on a holiday eve seemed uncertain.

A young woman lived in a trailer overlooking the public access area, which was on a lonely road in a remote, sparsely populated area. Naturally, two wet, bedraggled men knocking on her door at such an hour frightened her, but we stood back at an unthreatening distance in the glow of her porch light and persuaded her to let us use her phone. She shoved her landline through the door and closed it over the cord. Our call went through just in time because the outfitter was assembling the Pike County Search and Rescue squad to find us.

"Man, you don't know how happy I am to see you guys," the outfitter effused when he arrived at the takeout. "I did NOT want to spend Thanksgiving eve on this river looking for y'all! I'm just glad it's not summer. At least y'all didn't have any snakes to worry about."

"Snakes?" Clark asked.

"Cottonmouths," I said. "This river's alive with them in warm weather. They like to get in bushes that hang over the water. If you brush up against a bush with a snake in it, a lot of times he'll fall down in the canoe with you. There's never a good time for that to happen, but it can get really dicey if it happens in the dark."

"Dicey? In what way?" Clark asked.

"Either you or the snake is coming out of that boat, and it's probably going to be you," I answered. "And the snake won't be far behind you."

"You got that shit right!" said the outfitter, who gladly took his cue to regale us with disastrous snake-in-the-boat tales.

Our outfitter was impressed that we managed to cover so much distance in the dark without tumping a canoe.

"I'm just glad you guys know what you're doing," he said. "The greenhorns are the ones that give me heartburn."

John Carter, who owned the canoe livery, once told me about a young reporter for a local newspaper who visited to write a feature story about canoeing the Caddo River.

"I knew it was going to be trouble when she showed up wearing Top-Siders and capris," Carter said. "That's not appropriate river wear."

There is a place upstream from the stretch that Clark and I floated where the river channel cuts to the left. A big metal arrow nailed to a tree pointed the correct direction. If you keep right, you'll dead-end about a half-mile back in a cove. The reporter dallied too long and did not see the arrow in the fading light. She abandoned her canoe at the dead end, walked through the woods to the highway, and thumbed a ride back to town. She did not notify Carter, who found his canoe the next day. The reporter's fate was a mystery until an article came out in the paper titled, "River of No Return!" It was a horror story, but devoted river rats loved it because they believed it dissuaded nonlocals from visiting the Caddo.

Our ecstatic driver relived that story and many others on the drive back to our vehicles at Glenwood. He had a bag phone, an early monstrosity that was housed in a pouch large enough to carry softball equipment. Between stories, Clark called his wife. He held the phone a few inches from his ear, but everyone in the van heard every word she said. They divorced shortly after.

Clark and I didn't speak again for sixteen years, not because of antipathy but because our careers took us in divergent paths. He contacted me in 2010 as a representative for a major marketing firm that handled a number of prominent hunting brands. Clark invited me on an Oklahoma turkey hunt to field test some of his clients' new products.

"About that float trip," I said haltingly when we reunited. "It's far too long in coming, but I am really sorry for my role in anything that came after."

"Sorry! For what?" Clark replied, laughing. "I should thank you. That's one of the biggest favors anyone ever did for me!"

Our destination was near Sweetwater, Oklahoma, in Roger Mills County, not far from where I killed my first turkey in October 1999. Our host was Willard Gilley, the gruff but affable proprietor of Sweetwater Creek Outfitters. After we stashed our gear in his cabin, Gilley showed us the properties he'd reserved for us to hunt. The first stop was on a high hill that looked over a natural gas well into a distant field. About half a mile from our promontory, an army of turkeys strolled toward their roost area next to Sweetwater Creek. I counted seven strutting gobblers, an equal number of jakes, and a harem of hens. There was no cover around that field, so it would be very hard to hunt.

Our next visit was to an area that Gilley recommended for midday hunting. We couldn't see it in the dark, but Gilley said it was a scrub oak bottom covering several acres where turkeys loaf and eat grit in the heat of the day. Gilley showed us two other areas he said would be good in late afternoon and early evening. One was in a dense scrub oak bottom near a cow pasture.

"You don't see many mature gobblers in there, but the jakes and hens will cover you up," Gilley said. "If you can wait them out, a big one might sneak in there."

At the end of the tour, we sat atop a hill and gazed at the twinkling lights atop the generators at the Red Hills Wind Farm. The night was cool and windy. An angry cloud bank boiled up from the west as lightning flickered in the thunderheads. It was merely a western Oklahoma temper tantrum that grumbled and settled down without incident after speaking its piece. The sky would regain its good humor in the morning, and tomorrow would be a marvelous day to hunt turkeys.

Our first morning hunt was eventful but frustrating. We took the wrong route into the field before dawn, got lost, and then reoriented long after the turkeys were on the ground. We were behind the flock when we finally relocated it, with no discreet way to loop in front. We eventually got on the flock's flank at a range of about 200 yards. Two big gobblers displayed to our calls, but we could not persuade them to leave their hens. Eventually, they faded into a thicket. Not knowing their bearing, we aborted the chase.

We went driving at about 9 a.m., to check out the other properties. I leaned back in the passenger seat, stuffed a jacket under my head, and started drifting off to sleep as Clark punched up a song on his iPod that I hadn't heard in nearly thirty years. Mark Farner's harmonic finger taps in the intro to "Shinin' On" were unmistakable. I slowly raised an eyelid.

"Are you serious? Grand Funk Railroad?" I asked.

Clark smiled and said, "You're the only person I know who knows that song."

"I knew there was a reason I like you. Any Grand Funk fan is a friend of mine!" I crowed.

The rest of the morning was all about music. Clark and I have hunted together many times since, and "Shinin' On" is our battle hymn. With the music blasting, we commiserated over the morning's failure while driving through a veritable forest of wind turbines.

"I knew we were screwed the minute we got to that creek that wasn't supposed to be there," I lamented. "Something always seems to go wrong when I try to call birds down off the roost. All it means is that we get to hunt a little longer today. My best hunts have always been from eleven to one. That's when turkeys go into the shady bottoms, and they'll definitely do that today to get out of this wind."

At about 9:30 a.m., we saw seven turkeys dawdling in a field along a creek edge. Two gobblers strutted in the open about forty yards from the creek. With their fans and feathers puffed out in the wind, they looked like Spanish galleons under sail. I estimated the bigger gobbler's distance at 400 yards. Clark, who often hunts deer in that country, said it was closer to 800 yards. I'll split the difference and say it was most likely around 600. There was no cover, so the only approach was from the creek.

The water was shin deep where I entered, but the pools in the creek bends were knee deep to thigh deep. I was so excited that I didn't notice the cold, but I resented the certainty of enduring wet feet for the rest of the day. I sloshed upstream, stooping to keep my head and shoulders below the bank. When I encountered holes that were too deep, I skirted them on the low bank and fouled my gloves, cuffs, and elbows with sand burrs.

Several times I peeked over the bank to check on the gobbler. He was still strutting, oblivious to my approach. My final check revealed that I needed to go only fifty more yards to gain even with him. That was about the distance of a narrow sandspit sloping gently into the creek. A thin line of cottonwood trees and high grass was at the top. If I got there in time, I could crawl up the slope and pop the gobbler at a range of about thirty yards.

With my back and shoulders burning, I reached the sandspit. I was halfway up the bank when a hen appeared above me about fifteen feet away, doubtless to investigate the splashing noises coming from the creek. She looked at me. She looked to the left, and then to the right. Then she looked at me again.

"Putt!"

"Aw, piss!" I hissed.

The hen dashed back into the field, putt-putting frantically. I scrambled to the top of the bank, only to see my gobbler sprint to a distant fence and vanish into an adjacent field of tall grass. I sighed as my shoulders sagged. Clark was right. It was at least 800 yards back to the truck.

About thirty minutes later, we arrived at the oak bottom where Gilley said we would see jakes and hens. The draw was problematic. Either there was too much cover or too little. At the bottom of the draw was a wide, sunlit opening where I placed a decoy with its flanks facing both hillsides.

When I turned back to the woods, I spied a 55-gallon, blue plastic drum lying on its side. It was in the only spot that offered a clear view to the top of the draw and to the two funnels at the bottom of the draw. If a gobbler appeared anywhere in sight of the barrel, he would be in range. The barrel did not provide cover, and though it was a glaring and conspicuous feature, I reasoned that turkeys were accustomed to it and would not notice a camouflaged figure sitting beside it.

More important, that barrel gave me a curious combination of confidence and optimism. Through the years I have encountered trees that exuded such intense positivity that I was certain I would kill turkeys or deer sitting against them. I call them "magic" trees. Now, I had a magic barrel.

"We're going to get us a bird right here. I guarantee it," I said, parroting Joe Namath's brash 1968 prediction that his New York Jets would beat the heavily favored Baltimore Colts in Super Bowl III. It was a rash and silly thing for him to say, until he did it.

To prevent a turkey from sneaking in behind us, Clark sat about sixty yards away facing out toward a field. With my back against the barrel, I lowered my face mask and blew a series of yelps on my Woodhaven Copperhead diaphragm. Five minutes later, I saw movement in my periphery. A gobbler materialized in the brush on the hillside. It started toward me but then ran away. A second gobbler appeared, but it fled as well.

Those two turkeys sparked the hot wire of my chronic hunting-inadequacy syndrome. Evidently I was wrong about blending in with the blue barrel, and now I was powerless to adjust. More to the point, that hunt was likely ruined as well.

"What the hell are you thinking?" I asked myself. "You look like a Christmas ornament sitting beside this barrel! Dammit, boy, you come up with some stupid ideas sometimes!"

A bigger problem was that there was no place else to sit. As I flogged myself with recrimination, the real reason for the turkeys' reticence materialized. I didn't spook them. They were afraid of two bigger, burlier gobblers that were trailing them. The upgraded gobblers saw the decoy and stopped. My mind immediately sharpened on the mission. I froze and purred softly on my diaphragm. The first gobbler came in on a string, and I crumpled him at twenty yards with two ounces of No. 6 Hevi Shot. He was gorgeous, weighing in at twenty-two pounds and sporting a ten-inch beard with one-inch spurs. He didn't flop at all, and his quick death probably cost me.

Instead of fleeing, the second gobbler glared at his lifeless companion. I prepared to bag a double, which was then legal in Oklahoma. After a long stare, the second gobbler swung wide around his fallen comrade just out of range and vanished into the far thicket. If my bird had flopped, his buddy would probably have pounced on him. I could have poured a cup of coffee and eaten a donut unnoticed.

Unlike Eastern wild turkeys, which have brown-tipped tail feathers and bronze barring, the Rio Grande turkey has buff-tipped feathers and bluish-green barring. However, my bird had tips that were almost white, like a Merriam's turkey. Its feathers glowed like patina-tinged copper in the soft sunlight.

With the wind in his face and his hearing degraded from decades of hanging around in blues bars, Clark did not hear the shot. He was puzzled when he emerged from his spot to find me rising from behind the blue barrel with a gobbler slung over my shoulder.

As we exited the hollow, Gilley waited in his truck at the top of the hill, smoking a cigarette under the shade of a big tree.

"Lookie here, Willard! I rubbed a barrel to see if there was a genie inside, and this great big sumbitch came out!" I said.

"That's a nice bird," Gilley said in a raspy voice as he exhaled a smoke cloud. "Big damn bird!"

"I've got two more wishes," I said. "I wish that my buddy and I tag out."

That wish almost came true. Hunting together in a pop-up blind at a different location, we called up a pair of two-year-old gobblers that strolled in together.

"On the count of three, I'll shoot the one on the left, and you take the one on the right," I said. On "three," I shot my gobbler, but Clark flinched at my gun's report and missed his shot. However, he redressed that issue the next morning when he killed a gobbler before we had to return home. Thus began our mutual love affair with western Oklahoma turkey hunting.

CHAPTER ELEVEN

MASTERPIECE THEATER

I n the years when Arkansas turkeys eluded me, the combination of Glenn Clark and Oklahoma was like a salve.

I made so many unforced errors in the 2012 Arkansas spring season that I considered quitting the sport. My hiatus would have been short lived, of course. The pull was too strong, but ineptitude tainted my joy. A relentless stream of negative reinforcement had made turkey hunting tedious. After one particularly downcast outing, I asked myself if I sincerely enjoyed turkey hunting, or did I do it merely because it was a tacit job requirement? When you don't hear gobblers, the odds are squarely stacked against you, but I didn't even get an opportunity to misplay any birds. I might as well have been hunting ivory-billed woodpeckers.

At the nadir of my discontent, I landed the lead role in a masterpiece.

Clark, an account representative for a major promotional agency, invited me to one of our biennial hunts in western Oklahoma. As soon as we got on the road, Clark christened the quest when he punched up our war song, "Shinin' On," by Grand Funk Railroad. Conversation flowed freely as we shared the highlights and lowlights of our lives since we last hunted together.

Clark, a relentless salesman, had recently bought a new Toyota Tundra pickup truck. For the next seven hours he chattered about the Tundra's fuel economy, towing capacity, horsepower rating, lumbar support, sound system, instrumentation, suspension, and everything else that helped make his life on the road more comfortable.

About ninety minutes before dark, Willard Gilley drove us to the new properties he'd reserved for us to hunt. As an outfitter, Gilley acquires new leases every year and lapses depleted or unproductive leases. He reserves properties for specific bookings to ensure clients don't interfere with one another and to ensure a high-quality experience. Gilley is also familiar with every gobbler that inhabits his leases.

When Gilley turns a hunter loose on a property, he says things like, "There's a longbeard that comes into this field from the bottom every day between two and three. If you can wait him out, you might have a good chance of seeing him."

Or, "A group of two-year-old gobblers goes through this little bottom every day about lunchtime. Nobody hunts the neighboring farms, so they don't get bothered coming or going."

Gilley's reports are not guide jive. They are eyewitness accounts.

For this tour, I rode shotgun in Gilley's battered old Chevrolet Silverado crew cab. Clark occupied the back seat.

"These old Chevys sure have a lot of character," I said. "This one has a classic, 'King Kong work truck' vibe. Makes you want to go build something. Or tear something down."

"It's kind of like me," Gilley said warily. "It's got some hard miles on it, but it keeps plugging along."

Raising my voice a little, I said, "Chevy's 5.3-liter motor is a workhorse. I bet it'll outrun Glenn's Toyota."

I caught Gilley's eye and winked.

"Out-pull it too," Gilley grunted, cupping his left hand against the side draft from the open window to light a cigarette.

"What?" Clark asked, affronted. "The five-seven in my Tundra has 381 horsepower and 401 pounds of torque, with a 7,700-pound towing capacity. Chevy doesn't have anything that comes close!"

"Wind him up, and watch him go," I murmured.

Gilley responded with a raspy chuckle as he blew smoke out the window.

The next morning, our first hunt started and ended like all of my 2012 Arkansas hunts. We arrived before sunrise at an abandoned homestead amid a grove of Osage orange and scrub oaks. Ground cover was sparse, so Clark and I sat together against a pair of wide trees with a cloth screen stretched before us. We had a clear view, but we counted on shadows and our low profiles to conceal our silhouettes.

After sunrise, I scratched a series of light tree yelps from a small slate call designed especially for that purpose. A nearby gobbler responded. Minutes later, a dark blob in front of an outstretched fan appeared in the shadows.

I clucked with my mouth call, and the gobbler approached in strut. He pranced three or four steps forward, pivoted, and pranced three or four steps to the side. His fan dipped and flashed as he pirouetted ever nearer. Even in the shadows, his head and wattles pulsed like a red and blue lava lamp. My racing heart and my awe watching that gobbler answered the first question. Yes, I enjoy turkey hunting very much, and I would do it zealously if it weren't part of my job.

The minutes it takes for a strutting gobbler to waltz into range are the most exhilarating, most nerve-wracking minutes in hunting. So many things can foil the game at the last moment. In this case, a pair of hens flew off the roost and landed about twenty-five yards to the gobbler's left. They peered our direction before leading the gobbler out through the other end of the shelterbelt. Clark and I scrambled around the windrow to get in front of the birds and cut them off, but they vanished as if they had gone through a trapdoor. They were still in the thicket, but it's futile to try to overtake turkeys from behind, and there was no cover to hide us for an attempt to maneuver in front of them. That hunt was done, but even in the pall of my disappointment, the answer to my question remained solid. I didn't just enjoy turkey hunting. I lived for it.

In the afternoon we went to a different place, an eighty-acre field that abuts a wooded creek bottom. Again sitting side by side, Clark and I called from a grassy thicket for nearly two hours until the wind finally grew insurmountable. As we stood to stretch, Clark said, "I kind of had my side to the field because I half expected one to try to slip in behind us."

"You had the right idea because there one is," I said.

A mature gobbler stared at us from the tall grass about thirty-five yards away. Incredulous, we didn't think to shoot the bird. With just three steps, it vanished into the waving grass. It reminded me of a lesson that Meadowlark Clark taught me years before in Missouri. Gobblers go to fields in the middle of the day. We got that part right, but this turkey surprised us by approaching from upwind in tall grass that muffled sound while creating its own white noise. I had believed that turkeys avoided white-noise generators like rustling grass because it dampens their ability to hear.

That taught me another lesson. A turkey can hear and pinpoint the origin of a call despite wind direction and distortion. Wind matters to hunters, but I don't believe it matters to turkeys.

We ended the day hunting a different property, on a natural gas right-of-way between two thickets. We entered the right-of-way by slipping under a barbed-wire fence surrounding a natural gas well. The barbs snagged my ghillie garments. Every movement to free myself ensnared me further, finally forcing me to wriggle out of my jacket and pants and unsnarl them independently.

Clark and I sat side by side in the stillness of the early evening. Behind us was a small rise covered by a thicket so dense that we believed it impossible for a creature to traverse it.

Several deer passed us, feeding placidly. They smelled us but did not discern our camouflaged forms.

Sight, sound, and smell are a deer's primary defense mechanisms. I have noticed that, generally, one sensory offense does not trigger a deer to flee. It takes at least two. If a deer smells you, it will try to provoke you to move. It sometimes walks almost to arm's length. If it hears or sees you, it moves with the wind to catch your scent. Two triggers complete the alarm circuit, and then it's game over.

I have long noticed that deer come closer to me in turkey season than they do when I am hunting deer with archery equipment. My clothing is the same. My scent is the same. The only thing different is my disposition toward the deer. I attribute the difference in their disposition toward me to what I call the "Aura of Bad Intentions."

Anybody who has ever walked on city streets has at some time experienced an inexplicable sensation of intense unease. It's a feeling of being watched, being sized up as prey. Instinctively, you become acutely attuned to your surroundings. Your head is on a swivel. Your gait quickens. You might even seek a crowd for the safety in numbers. It's not paranoia. Somebody probably was evaluating you as a potential victim. You sensed that person's predatory energy.

It's that way with wildlife too. I seldom see game when my predatory drive is in gear, but countless times I have gone to sleep while hunting or immersed myself in my smartphone, only to wake or return to awareness surrounded by deer or snap back to attentiveness by a turkey's cluck or gobble.

Distracted, I am a benign presence that does not emit an aura of bad intentions. I will go further and say that auras of bad intentions are species specific. When hunting turkeys, for example, I have no interest in deer and do not project predatory energy at them. I recall a deer hunt in Arkansas when a yearling buck that was not legal for me to shoot almost touched noses with me. It kept its eye on me as it continued up the hill, but it never became alarmed.

When turkey hunting, I have called up so many deer that I tried using the tactic in the fall for bowhunting, sort of like reverse psychology. It didn't work, I believe, because I truly had bad intentions for deer. I've noticed it with turkeys too. They often show up or sound off when I'm distracted with my phone.

Several hens crossed the right-of-way in front of Clark and me without noticing us as did a small flock of jakes later. Mainly from boredom, Clark and I clucked and yelped softly at each other and whispered compliments about each other's calls. Clark eventually stopped calling, but I continued. My hair stood atingle when a deep, questioning cluck rang from the thicket like a sonar ping from an old submarine war movie. It was clearly a gobbler, and it was pointless to respond. We were busted, and the gobbler putt-putted uneasily as it departed.

"How in the world could a bird get through that tangle?" I asked.

I got up to investigate. The cover immediately to our backs was hopelessly thick, but only for a few yards before it opened. The rise ascended to a small flat that was filthy with turkey sign. It was the gobbler's personal strutting parlor. More than just a perfunctory scan would have put us in position to bag what was surely a magnificent old gobbler. The revelation left me immediately disheartened and disgusted, but it was also instructive. In the future, I would scout well beyond what was immediately in view.

Clark and I got a late start the next morning, but we agreed that we would improve our chances hunting separately. I had a strong hunch that turkeys would be at the same property where the hayfield gobbler busted us the day before, but that place better suited Clark, who relies more on sight than sound. With the wind howling by midmorning, Clark set up in a gap connecting three fields, giving him a concealed view of multiple approach points.

I took the eighty acres across the road. It was mostly a weedy pasture with shinnery thickets dotting the top of a hill. Shinnery is a scrub oak, an oversized shrub, really, that grows in thickets called "motts." Shinnery produces a very small acorn that turkeys and quail love to eat.

Three rows of Osage orange formed a border on one side of the field. I considered setting up in the outer row but abstained because tall grass obscured my view of the field.

Leaving the far end of the shelterbelt, I crested the hill and descended into a narrow, wooded draw that curled like a ribbon below an open, grassy hill on the other side. The draw, a natural wildlife funnel, was the only decent place to hunt, but the ground cover was too dense. The spiny, spindly trees were too small to make backrests. The only place with a view was in the gap that split the woods at the bottom of the draw and connected the fields on both sides. The odds of encountering a turkey there were low.

Reversing course, I returned to the Osage orange grove. It was about 10 a.m., and true to Meadowlark Clark's observations, turkeys were in the field feeding toward the top of the hill near a derelict barn. They ignored my calls, so I leaned against an Osage orange tree and watched them vanish over the crest.

I continued to the far corner of that field and entered a woodlot atop the hill. It was a light, airy grove of post oaks and black oaks between two fields. It was a protected conduit for turkeys, but the sparse amount of turkey sign in that spot was old.

A high spot gave me a patchy view into the fields on both sides of the woodlot. I sent out feelers with several different calls, but the place felt inert. That put me in a familiar position. I always believe it's better "over there," and I constantly fight the impulse to move for the sake of merely being someplace else. A spot might feel inert now, but it can activate in a blink. How many opportunities have I cost myself by moving prematurely? How many turkeys have I spooked that came in silently when I dropped my guard? A bunch, for sure.

On the other hand, sometimes it really is better "over there." How many opportunities have I lost by trying to bluff a win from a bad hand? That's happened a bunch too. I live by instinct and feel. I had to find a place that made me feel better.

My options were limited, but I couldn't get the wooded draw out of my mind. Despite its many demerits, it was a pinch point for any wildlife moving between the fields or through the woods. It was my only legitimate play. I would figure out the rest.

Uphill from the wooded draw is an archipelago of shinnery motts. The motts are about fifteen to thirty yards long. The interiors of the motts are impenetrable for people, but you can sneak around the edges from one to the other and be shielded from the sight of anything on the other side. The brush is too tall to see over the top, but you can see through the branches on the edges. The last mott in the chain overlooks the wooded draw from about eighty yards. There was no other cover between them.

As I rounded the tip of the mott, I saw a gobbler sitting in the shade at the edge of the gap in the draw. Its head was retracted and at rest. I backed up behind the mott, but I feared that the bird saw me. I inched toward the tip and peered through low branches. The turkey remained prone and relaxed. I ducked back behind the thick cover and yelped with my mouth call. I inched forward and peered through the branches. The gobbler was still down, but its head was high and its expression alert.

I backed up and yelped again. I inched forward and peered through the branches. The gobbler was afoot and looking for the origin of the sound.

I backed up and yelped again. The tom gobbled. I responded, and the tom double-gobbled. I peered through the branches. The tom was in partial display. I belted out a couple of cutts, and the tom began strutting up the hill. He was committed. The only question was around which end of the mott he would come.

The gobbler vanished for several minutes, and my head swiveled as I tried to watch both ends of the mott. When the gobbler reappeared, he was only thirty yards away and approaching my end. His head glowed red, white, and blue as he bobbed in and out of view through the leafy branches. His fan was outstretched and seemed to fill the small windows through the foliage. He took a few final steps and cleared the end of the mott. We stood face to face, about eight feet apart. The gobbler's expression was unmistakable. He knew he was in deep trouble.

It's hard to believe you can miss a big target with a shotgun at eight feet, but I did. As the gobbler sprinted back down the hill, I aimed at the base of his neck and fired another round from the Mossberg 930 semi-automatic. A triplex load of 5-6-7 Hevi Shot dropped him at a range of about twenty-five yards. He was a big-bodied tom with a 9 ½-inch beard and ⅞-inch spurs.

Battered by a near gale, Clark's spot was a morass of swaying grass and white noise that made it nearly impossible to see or hear a turkey. I felt I had wrung all I could from my field across the road, so we relocated to a much calmer spot in a grassy bottom along the North Fork of the Red River in Beckham County. While Clark took care of business on his smartphone, a gobbler that was almost identical to the one I killed earlier in the day strolled in front of my gun. Its beard was thicker, but it was just nine inches long. Its spurs also were ⅞ of an inch.

On the drive home, I reflected on the extremes of the season. I misplayed the few decent opportunities I had in Arkansas and ended the season without firing a shot. In Oklahoma, I played my hands adroitly in games that were much more fluid and dynamic.

Maybe I was more comfortable hunting in prairies than in woods. Rio Grande gobblers are reputedly easier to hunt than Eastern birds. Maybe Eastern birds were beyond my abilities. I rejected both notions. Hunting Rio Grande birds is different, but Rios are not easier. Justified or not, Eastern gobblers are the standard for difficulty, and Easterns are my home birds.

One thing was for certain. I was much better at improvisational hunting and spontaneous adaptation. That's hunting's version of the spread offense. My tactics in Arkansas were static. Sit and wait. Three yards and a cloud of dust. I am comfortable playing that game, but turkeys are defensive specialists. It takes versatility to score against them.

I had proven that I can win on the road, but a champion wins at home. Mastering Arkansas turkeys was my next frontier, and I returned home with renewed confidence and resolve.

CHAPTER TWELVE

A PERFECT DAY

I f I could bottle the recipe for a perfect day, it would look, feel, sound, and taste like April 21, 2013.

In that era, good turkey hunting days were scarce in Arkansas. Perfect days were mythical. Arkansas had once been a turkey hunting mecca, but its turkey population crashed after a record spring turkey harvest in 2003. While hunters killed too many gobblers in the bountiful years, biologists cited bad weather as a turkey's biggest enemy for most of the early 2000s. A string of cold, wet springs and prolonged periods of extreme flooding during the hatching and brood-rearing season devastated turkey reproduction.

The White River National Wildlife Refuge, the only significant amount of turkey habitat in southeast Arkansas inland of the Mississippi River levees, was largely submerged each spring for nearly ten years, drowning any significant turkey production. The same was true for many of the islands along the Mississippi River, like Jackson Point and Woodstock. As a result, spring harvests fell from nearly 20,000 gobblers in 2004 to less than 7,000 in 2021.

To brake the skid, the Arkansas Game and Fish Commission (AGFC) took several significant actions that were designed to reduce hunter impact. In 2009, the AGFC permanently closed fall turkey season. Adult hunters have been prohibited from killing jakes since 2011. Also in 2011, the AGFC shortened spring turkey season to sixteen days, compared to thirty-seven days in 2003. In 2017, the AGFC changed opening day of spring turkey season to Monday instead of the traditional Saturday, again to reduce hunting pressure on adult gobblers.

There were pulses of recovery in 2010, 2012, and 2020, when springs were dry and warm. Nesting conditions and brood rearing conditions were excellent. Turkeys profited from the AGFC's adjustments, but hunting was so bad for so long that many Arkansans quit pursuing turkeys in their home state. Failure to hear even one gobble in a season discouraged many of our state's most accomplished turkey hunters.

Because of the paucity of birds and the short season, it was, and still is, a big accomplishment to kill a gobbler in Arkansas. That was the backdrop of the 2013 season, which for me began an extended period of accelerated maturity and success.

A key figure in this progression is Mike Stanley, pastor of Friendship Baptist Church in Highland, Arkansas. Stanley pastored the church for more than thirty years, shepherding a flock whose members live in seven counties in Arkansas and Missouri. The average tenure of a Baptist pastor is about four years.

As a charter member of the Arkansas Game and Fish Commission's volunteer chaplain corps, Stanley frequently counsels and comforts families of hunting, boating, and diving victims, often while recovery efforts are in progress. I have seen him take phone calls while hunting to counsel and comfort troubled and bereaved parishioners. He is a dedicated and committed servant, but he is also a gold medal turkey hunter.

Stanley and I met in 2008 when he emailed me his thoughts about one of my newspaper columns. Discussions soon turned to mutual personal interests like our families, and eventually to turkey hunting. Stanley invited me to hunt with him and his son Micaiah that year in Sharp County, a remote portion of the eastern Ozarks in the heart of Arkansas's most prosperous turkey country. We worked a tenacious old gobbler that Micaiah named "Woody," but at that stage of my career, I was no match for a bird of Woody's stature.

From that point on, "Brother Mike" became one of my most influential mentors. Through him I also met Philip Pickett, an Arkansas State Police trooper based in northern Arkansas who is well known in his community for taking youngsters on their first turkey hunts. I have spent hours on the phone with Stanley and Pickett, gleaning advice about how to manage the various scenarios that turkey hunters encounter.

Conversations with Pickett often become newspaper and magazine articles. Stanley prefers to stay out of print, but he will talk for hours off the record about turkey-calling tactics. When we're not talking, we're exchanging text messages, often while hunting and sometimes while working gobblers.

One important lesson Stanley taught me is that a hunter doesn't really react to anything a gobbler does because reaction empowers a gobbler to dictate the terms of the engagement. An assertive hunter dictates the terms by positioning and calling. He forces the gobbler to react, and then he adapts to a gobbler's reaction.

Stanley's specialty is the "fighting purr," an aggressive call that simulates the vocalizations of two turkeys fighting. It is a loud, frenetic call that works best if a partner is present to beat a turkey wing against his leg and against the ground. Stanley says it is the secret weapon that often closes the deal on the most recalcitrant gobblers. I carry two calls especially for this purpose. They are thin wooden boxes containing small blocks that you push back and forth with your thumbs. You control volume and pitch by thumb pressure. With one in each hand, they make a formidable fighting purr.

About that same time, I also met two other key mentors: Bill Rhodes of Sheridan, Arkansas, and Eddie Horton of Camden, Arkansas. A retired Army Corps of Engineers employee, Rhodes is a fanatical turkey hunter who makes distinctive box calls. He specializes in working with uncommon woods like chinaberry, zebrawood, and even mahogany. Rhodes made me a call from chinquapin, a western relative of the American chestnut that, like its cousin, was driven virtually extinct by chestnut blight. Chinquapin wood is rare, and that call is a prized possession.

I bought my first Rhodes box in 2011 after my employer gave me a bonus for winning the Freedom of Information Award from the Arkansas Press Association. The award was for a series of articles I wrote exposing an illegal attempt by the Arkansas Game and Fish Commission to subvert the Arkansas Freedom of Information Act by implementing its own freedom of information policy. The Arkansas Bar Association also gave me its Customer Service Award for the same articles, an honor that it bestows only when the organization believes it is warranted. Griffin Smith, our executive editor at that time, said that award winners must buy something personal with award bonuses.

"It is an unwritten rule that you are not to pay bills with it," Smith said.

I bought three Rhodes calls and reviewed them favorably in a column. Though we had not met, Rhodes reciprocated by making me a custom, dual-chamber model from cedar that has proven to be one of my most effective calls. A dual-chamber call is so difficult to make and to tune that Rhodes made only a few experimental models before abandoning the effort. He gets furious every time I write about it because readers flood him with requests that he can't fill.

In his shop, Rhodes taught me the art of using a box call, especially how to make it purr. He also taught me the tonal nuances of different woods and how they relate to different woodland environments. I like a walnut call when hunting in hardwoods, and I like laminates for hunting in open environments because of the way they project sound.

"If you had to have just one, you can't ever go wrong with a simple cedar box," Rhodes said. "It's the most versatile of them all."

Like Rhodes, Eddie Horton uses uncommon woods and laminates in unique, patented designs that cover every inch of the sonic palette. A Rhodes caller is deep, full-throated, and raspy. Horton's callers are clear and resonate. They are not inherently raspy, but you can make them produce a raspy "bite" on demand. My favorite is a laminate model called the "Arkansas Razorbox." Like Rhode's dual-chamber, Horton no longer makes the Razorbox, and I rankle him whenever I write about it as well.

Whenever I show interest in a particular call, Horton snatches it from my hand, raises it close to his left ear, belts out a few cutts, and finishes with a yelping sequence. He closes his eyes, shudders theatrically, and growls a protracted, two-syllable, "MmmM!" The accent is on the second "M." It's the same reaction a southern man elicits when he takes the first bite of an exceptional pecan pie. It seals the deal for wavering customers.

"I've played tug-of-war with many a customer trying to yank it back away from me," Horton said, laughing. "If you try to take it away from him, it makes him want it that much more!"

Horton taught me how to make a box call purr with only one hand. The technique enables me to manipulate pitch and direction by working the call next to my thigh at ground level or even behind my back. The modulations can disarm the most reticent gobbler's defenses. With their distinctive disparate tones and timbres, having a Rhodes box and a Horton box in the vest is a devastating one-two punch.

Three more important characters are Patrick Frachiseur of Dierks, Arkansas; David Taylor of Sheridan, Arkansas; and Grant Westmoreland of Sheridan, Arkansas. Frachiseur, owner of Premium Game Calls, makes all types of calls, but I am fond of his Diamond Cutter pot call and his diaphragms. Taylor makes fantastic friction calls featuring chinaberry frames with slate and copper surfaces. The secret to his calls is his incomparable strikers.

Westmoreland, an insurance agent, is politically conservative and supports conservative politicians and causes. However, he was also a staunch ally and supporter of Mike Ross, a Democrat who long represented Arkansas's Fourth Congressional District before running unsuccessfully for governor in 2014. Ross retired from politics following that campaign.

I actually met Ross before I met Westmoreland in quite an unconventional fashion on March 29, 2009. I was home alone, in the abyss of chemotherapy and radiation treatment for colorectal cancer. I was sick, sore, depressed, and bored that evening when I answered a call on my landline phone. A recorded voice invited me to participate in a telephone town hall meeting with Ross that was about to begin. Well, why not? I didn't have anything better to do.

I punched the button combination to join the meeting. The voice then asked if I had a question for the congressman. I punched "star-3" for "Yes," fully doubting I would actually get a chance to speak.

After Ross answered a couple of questions, a live voice told me I was next in line to ask my question. To my great surprise, I was cued to ask Ross his opinion about House Resolution 45—the Blair Holt Bill—which would have required gun owners to register all firearms that had an external feeding device.

Ross answered the question with an astonishing level of candor and sincerity.

"HR-45 has been referred to the House Judiciary committee where it has received no co-sponsors," Ross replied. "Usually, if it's a good idea, people join on as co-sponsors, and nobody has done so. I'm opposed to HR-45, and I'm going to make sure it dies in committee."

Unprompted, Ross also explained his opposition to reinstating the Brady Gun Ban, which was a hot issue in 2009.

"We all know that didn't work, and that's why I helped lead the effort to make sure it was not reinstated when it expired in 2004," Ross said. "We had sixty-five pro-gun Democrats write a letter to the attorney general saying we're opposed to it, and I am going to lead the effort to defeat it."

Ross's comments were newsworthy, but there was some question as to whether they were fair game since I did not identify myself as a member of the media. On the other hand, I didn't call Ross. He called me, and I had no reason to believe he would have commented differently to a media member than to an unaffiliated constituent. I reasoned that he surely assumed that the media was listening to a live town hall meeting and that he intended for his comments to be reported. As far as I was concerned, I covered the meeting. That's how I justified it in a conference with our editorial director after I wrote a column about the exchange.

I wrote about the exchange with Ross in the voice of a sports fan calling a radio sports call-in program. I identified myself as "The Striper Sniper from Hot Spring County. Long-time listener, first-time caller."

I closed the piece with, "Good take, Congressman. One more thing: How many games do you think the Hogs [Arkansas Razorbacks] will win this year, and do you think they'll go to a BCS [Bowl Championship Series] bowl? I'll hang up and listen."

Three days later my phone rang again.

"Is this Bryan Hendricks?" asked a vaguely familiar voice.

"It is," I replied cautiously.

"This is Mike Ross. I just wanted to answer your last two questions. First, the Razorbacks will win eight or nine games this year. They probably won't go to a BCS bowl game, but they'll get invited to a good bowl. I think they'll go to a BCS bowl the year after next."

After we shared a rowdy laugh, Ross talked at even greater length about the ill-fated Blair Holt Bill, and I published his comments in a follow-up column. Both of Ross's football predictions were correct. The Razorbacks won eight games in 2009, and they played in the 2011 Sugar Bowl against Ohio State, their only BCS bowl appearance.

Not long after, I met Westmoreland, who was helping raise funds for Arkansas Hunters Feeding the Hungry, a nonprofit organization that encourages hunters to donate deer and other game to provide meals for nutrition-insecure Arkansans. Our introductory conversation veered to turkey hunting, spawning a new friendship.

In 2010, I accompanied Ross and Westmoreland on a crappie fishing trip at DeGray Lake near Arkadelphia, Arkansas. Ross talked at great length about the criticism he received from constituents when he cast the deciding vote that advanced the Affordable Care Act, President Barack Obama's signature accomplishment, out of committee to the floor of the House of Representatives. He also described the criticism he received from members of his party when he voted against the ACA in the general floor vote. It was one of the most fascinating conversations I have ever had while fishing or hunting.

Though an avid duck and deer hunter, Ross doesn't hunt turkeys. That seems to make even more discordant his friendship with Westmoreland, an accomplished turkey hunter who has taught me a lot about tactics and calling. He talks, I listen. He began making his own pot calls in 2017, and he gave me "No. 8." It is an excellent call that has assisted in the demise of a couple of gobblers.

I treasure these calls because of their personal connections and their various backstories. All of those people are friends and mentors. As strange as it sounds, I hear their voices in the calls. When I use a Rhodes call, I hear Bill's syrupy south Arkansas accent telling me exactly the speed and angle to sweep the lid. Horton's calls evoke his gruff, plainspoken attitude. I hear that "pecan pie" exclamation every time I finish a yelp sequence, and I believe it sounds like pecan pie to gobblers too. Whenever I look at or hear a Premium Game Call, I see Patrick Frachiseur's trademark Stetson hat. Westmoreland's No. 8 call projects the smooth, glib voice of a master salesman.

Their underlying attraction to me is that they are made in Arkansas by Arkansas craftsmen. My motto is "Arkansas callers for Arkansas gobblers," but I always take them on the road too. If they can call up a wily old Arkansas tom, they'll call up gobblers anywhere.

Some of these calls were in my vest on opening day of the 2013 spring turkey season. It was thirty-six degrees at home and thirty-four degrees at the gate of my hunting lease in Grant County. It wasn't yet 5 a.m. when I reached my jumping off point, which gave me plenty of time to sip my coffee and inventory my gear. My kit included five slate calls: a Knight & Hale Yella Hammer, a Premium

Game Calls Aluminum Cutter, a Premium Game Calls Diamond Cutter Legend, an H.S. Strut Lil' Deuce, and a call of unknown manufacture. That last one is an heirloom. Inside the clear glass is a breast feather of a Rio Grande gobbler over rough slate. One-third of the glass is a textured calling surface. On the bottom, in a recess, is the smooth bottom of the slate disc. The call changes pitch and timbre by using the top or bottom.

Additionally, in one pocket was a walnut Rhodes box that makes a deep, raspy tone. In another pocket was my first Horton laminated call, which has a high, clear, and dulcet tone. I also had a big boat paddle of a box bearing the logo of the Arkansas Game and Fish Foundation and the Arkansas Game and Fish Commission's mission statement. It was a gift from the late Steve Smith, the longtime president of the Arkansas Game and Fish Foundation and a longtime member of the Arkansas State Police Commission. Smith was a good friend and a consummate gentleman, as well as a font of wisdom and institutional knowledge about the Game and Fish Foundation, the Game and Fish Commission's lobbying and fundraising auxiliary.

Smith's call is monstrous, and I considered it more a conversation piece than a serious turkey call. It squeals, with an overtone that sounds almost like electric guitar feedback. When I finally figured out how to work it, it proved very useful. A light stroke makes it howl. It is ideal for calling in high wind and across long distances.

In yet another pocket was a Sam Pope Pock'et Call made by Chattahoochee Game Calls. It sounds like a young hen, and it often gets a tom to gobble when nothing else will. I also had a Primos push-button yelper and a Woodhaven Red Wasp mouth call.

I carried all those calls for several reasons. My vest has a lot of pockets, and an empty pocket is a wasted pocket. Also, I wanted to have the right call for any situation I encountered. A box or a slate sounds one way in the house, but it often sounds entirely different in the woods. Some calls sound better in hardwood forests. Others sound better among pines, and others are better for fields. I learned to exploit their individual strengths, and carrying a large selection gave me confidence. Also, multiple calls represent multiple hens. If one hen entices a gobbler, I reason that multiple hens entice him more.

Mainly, having that many calls was kind of a security blanket for a fragile, insecure, and relatively inexperienced hunter. I couldn't bring every call I had, but I could bring a bunch, and surely one of them would make the right sound at the right time. It was the one aspect of turkey hunting I could control, and it eliminated a source of potential anxiety.

Weighed down by this veritable sporting goods aisle of squeaking, clacking turkey callers, I entered the woods on April 21, 2013, long before daylight and padded down a logging trail to my hunting spot. The footing was slick, and a Christmas ice storm had deposited a tangle of limbs and small trees across the path. I had just settled down against a tree when the sounds of tires crunching on distant gravel announced that the season had begun. Two men made owl hoots as they entered woods on a neighboring club. They sounded more like inebriated fans at an Eric Church concert. No birds gobbled, which I found both gratifying and unsettling.

The first turkey gobbled at about 6:30 a.m. Four others chimed in. They were all on the ground. Not a single bird gobbled from the roost. One bird came quickly and gobbled continuously. I believed it was the same loquacious bird I called up as a jake on opening day 2012. It got to within seventy-five yards and stopped on the trail. The tom turned north and gobbled as its volume faded. A shot sounded from that direction, and the gobbling ceased. I heard the last gobble at about 7:15 a.m.

At about 9 a.m., I went to town for breakfast and to visit a sporting goods store where I encountered a gray, camouflage ghillie poncho, a mesh garment festooned with hundreds of fabric bits that gives its wearer the appearance of a bush. It takes only a few seconds to put the thing on, providing instant cover to a turkey hunter or enabling a turkey hunter to disappear into existing cover. I bought it. Hours later, it proved indispensable.

When I returned at noon, all the other hunters were gone. The air was cool, still, and crystalline. I knew exactly where I wanted to go. A little knoll in an oak flat juts into a big pine thicket and tapers gently into a creek bottom. I picked an open spot at the edge of a young pine thicket that overlooks the bottom. A cluster of cedar trees between the thicket and me formed a screen to absorb my silhouette. I planted a Primos She-Mobile hen decoy on a high point that was visible from the creek bottom. The afternoon sun illuminated its side. I put on the ghillie poncho and sat in my collapsible pack chair. I then made a few yelps and took a short nap.

When I awoke, I arrayed all my calls at my feet. For the next three hours, I worked each one in fifteen-minute intervals, but with no apparent effect. At about 4 p.m., I considered going home, but I was in no rush. The afternoon was delightful, and I felt content. As I scrolled through my social media account on my smartphone, footsteps in the leaves raised my hackles. Heavy and way too loud, they were approaching fast from the creek bottom.

Some damn fool hunter is stalking my calls, I thought angrily.

Stalking a call is extremely dangerous for the caller and the stalker, and it's a good way to get shot. It happened to a coworker at the Missouri Department of Conservation while hunting at a public hunting area. In 1987, Greg LeMond, the only American at that time to have won the Tour de France, was shot and nearly killed in a call-stalking incident in California. To mitigate the risk, I always wear Oakley sunglasses with prescription antiballistic lenses that will withstand a shotgun blast. If I ever get shot in the face, at least I won't lose my eyes.

Resisting the urge to shout a warning, I looked for movement. The footfalls came from a dense thicket of briars, brush, and honeysuckle. It was an unlikely place for a person to walk. Armadillos and squirrels sound like bulldozers when they root through the leaves, but this was a purposeful, bipedal gait.

I was dumbstruck to see not a hunter, but a pair of mature, broom-bearded gobblers striding in lockstep. They vanished momentarily in a shallow draw, giving me a couple of seconds to mount my shotgun. Neither tom made a peep, but the lead gobbler emerged from the draw and trotted to the decoy, oblivious to the ghillie-clad blob that sat almost within tackling distance. The second gobbler was the same size, but with a slightly shorter beard. I couldn't shoot without hitting both toms, which is illegal in Arkansas. The season bag limit is two, but you cannot kill two turkeys on the same day.

The toms circled the decoy, but they were still too close together. *Come on, man, move!* I silently begged the subordinate gobbler, my arms burning under the shotgun's weight.

It moved directly behind the bigger gobbler.

Aww, you sorry son of a . . . Get out from behind him, dadgum you! I thought.

Finally, the subordinate tom stepped to the side as the bigger bird suspiciously eyed the decoy. It stood erect and twitched its head indecisively. One shot from my Winchester SX3, which replaced my SX2, rolled the tom at about fifteen yards. As I clambered to subdue the thrashing gobbler, the uninjured turkey stood frozen. He took a few seconds to react, but even then he merely trotted away, "putt-putting" with increasing tempo. In a breath, he vanished into the brush. The gobblers were probably nest mates that had never spent a minute apart. In a flash, the survivor was on his own.

The time was 4:13 p.m., a magic number that exemplifies the glory of late afternoon hunting.

I took a knee and said a prayer of thanksgiving. Then I tagged my bird, placed it beside a sun-drenched oak log, and gazed in awe at its shimmering bronze feathers. The soft pastels of the April oak foliage filtered the early evening light as if through emerald and gold-stained glass. I sat for about twenty minutes soaking in the sights, sounds, and smells of the moment. I texted photos to my friends and basked in their congratulations.

Driving home, I stopped at a country grocery store and asked a customer getting into his car if the store had a scale on which I could weigh a turkey.

"Not many turkeys around these parts," said the man dismissively. "What'd you get?"

I extracted the gobbler from the back seat of my crew cab truck and hoisted it by the legs. Its wings and beard cascaded toward the pavement.

"Big bird!" the man exclaimed. "Damn nice bird! You kill that around here?"

"Up the road a bit," I replied.

The guy closed his car door, about-faced, and escorted me into the store. He asked the manager, his friend, if I could weigh the bird on the store's meat scale. It weighed only 15 ½ pounds, but its beard was 10 ⅞ inches long. The spurs were ⅞-inch long.

I called Mike Stanley, who insisted on hearing every detail. In that moment, our relationship crossed the student-teacher threshold into the realm of peers.

In my world, a perfect day looks just like that.

CHAPTER THIRTEEN

THE BOSS

Old Belfast Hunting Club encompasses about 4,400 acres lying fourteen miles south of Benton, Arkansas. It is the center of my hunting universe, but it's also a central part of my life.

Mike Romine invited me to join the club in March 2009, the month I began treatment for colorectal cancer. I met Romine, an employee for a big natural gas utility, in 2005 when he organized a dove hunt to benefit Arkansas Children's Hospital. Our bond was instant, but it quickly transcended to something nearer to brotherhood.

After a landowner orientation for the dove hunt, I drove to the hunting grounds with Romine and his brother-in-law, Barry Peel.

"Everybody got their hunting license and HIP permit?" Peel asked.

Anyone who hunts migratory birds in the United States must possess a free Harvest Information Program permit, or HIP. The annual permit enables the U.S. Fish and Wildlife Service to determine how many people hunt migratory birds and provides a rough estimate of how many migratory birds they kill in a year. In the whirl of pre-hunt preparations, I forgot to get mine.

"Looks like I'll only be shooting photos today," I said dejectedly.

After getting his gear from the truck, Peel handed me his keys.

"Run into town, and get legal," Peel said.

134

In the South, a man's pickup truck is inviolable. Handing your keys to another man is like saying, "Take my girlfriend out for the evening." Barry Peel entrusted his ride to me, a stranger, with the confidence usually reserved for close kin.

Peel's easygoing nature belied severe depression that he concealed from even his closest relations. It conquered him in late August 2012 while sitting in his favorite deer stand at Old Belfast. Romine was at the club, beginning work on a new box stand, when he drove past the entrance to an interior logging road where Romine and Peel kept elevated box stands. The gate was open. Interior road gates are locked if they aren't being used for logging, and no logging was occurring at that time. Romine turned to investigate and found Peel sitting inside his deer stand. Nobody sits inside a wooden box in the humid heat of late summer when deer season is closed. Peel was uncharacteristically aloof and eerily serene.

"He acted like he had something up there that he didn't want me to see," Romine said. "I didn't think too much of it. It wasn't any business of mine."

The two chatted amiably for a few minutes, and Romine continued on his way.

"The last thing he said was, 'I love you, brother. Y'all be careful out there,'" Romine said.

What Peel did not want Romine to see was the 20-gauge shotgun he held pressed against his leg. It was a break-action model capable of holding only one cartridge.

Minutes later, Peel sent a text message to Romine's son Zack Smith instructing him to call 911 and direct police to his deer stand on BB Road. Smith, who was at home, immediately perceived Peel's intent, He begged Peel to desist with frantic text messages.

"Please don't do this! We all love you!" Smith pleaded, but Peel did not respond.

In tears, Smith called Romine.

"That's bullshit!" argued Romine. "I was just with him not more than three minutes ago!"

Smith forwarded Peel's texts to Romine who spun his truck around and roared back to Peel's deer stand.

Peel shot himself in the chest with a solid lead slug. Romine's attempts to administer CPR were as gory as they were heroic. Each breath spewed blood, lung chunks, and bone fragments through the gaping wounds in Peel's chest and back, coating Romine from neck to waist. Romine held Peel as Peel's essence departed. When sheriff's deputies arrived, they questioned Romine intensely. The tension abated when a deputy found suicide notes in Peel's truck, the same truck he had lent me the day we met.

Bill Heavey, a columnist for *Field & Stream*, hunted deer with the Old Belfast Hunting Club that November, when the communal gash from Peel's death was still ragged and raw. Heavey described the pall that hovered over our camp when he shared his own battle with depression in the December 2019 issue of *Field & Stream*.

While Old Belfast retains its family atmosphere, it's never been the same since that awful day. It's as if there's a big hole in the air where Peel once dwelled. Romine created a small memorial containing Peel's ashes behind the camp at the edge of a cutover. The cutover has since grown into a thicket, and an impenetrable tangle of saw briars guards the memorial. You need a machete to reach it to avoid getting shredded. Someday it will mature into a beautiful, sun-drenched spot in the shade of tall pines as time ushers the earth through its seasons and cycles. We will all be old when the forest finally welcomes us back to Peel's resting place. Maybe then we can remember him without bitterness.

Meanwhile, Old Belfast makes new memories. My daughter Amy killed her only deer months after Peel's death as she sat beside me in Peel's stand. My late son, Daniel, was at my side when he killed his only deer on a different part of the property. Ten years later, Dan's chair in that stand remains beside mine. Sometimes I talk to it. My youngest daughter, Hannah, doesn't hunt, but she accompanies me on opening day of modern gun deer season to a spot called "The Thin." There's a certain holiness in a place that holds so many memories, in a place where you've shed so many tears and conversed so earnestly with your maker.

Though primarily a deer hunting property, Old Belfast is more important to me for turkey hunting. It took me several years to figure out turkey patterns in my section of the woods, and I quickly came to appreciate that I had a world-class hunting spot. That realization began the day a flock of Old Belfast turkeys taught me a valuable lesson.

While hunting on a natural gas right-of-way in 2010, I saw three dark shapes far in the distance. A long look through binoculars confirmed that they were turkeys, but I could not determine their sex. I slipped into the brush at the side of the right-of-way, backed up to the only big tree that offered a view of the opening, and scratched out a few yelps on a slate.

About twenty minutes later, I saw the turkeys through the branches. They were hens, and one poked her head into the brush three feet from my face. As far distant as they were when I called, they precisely pinpointed the source of the call. That proved to me that if a turkey can hear you, it knows exactly where you are. If it wants to find you, it will.

Before 2020, when the coronavirus pandemic created a new legion of turkey hunters, there were only four turkey hunters among forty-four members, and we each believed that's three too many. We know where each other hunts, and we stay out of one another's way. We do not speak to one another during the season. We become sociable again after the season ends, when we congratulate our successes and console our misfortunes.

Every turkey hunter has one career-defining bird, a graduate-level nemesis that stretches the limits of skill, patience, and endurance. Mine was an Old Belfast veteran I call The Boss.

We first met on April 19, 2014, opening day of the Arkansas spring turkey season. Like 2013, opening day was gorgeous in the rolling pine hills of northern Grant County. Buoyed by my success on opening day of 2013, I started the day as confidently as Union Gen. Irvin McDowell started the First Battle of Bull Run. Expecting a rout, I rolled onto the battlefield on a bunting-draped shay serenaded by a drum and fife corps. It turned into a ten-day equivalent of Fredericksburg.

On opening day, I hunted a logging trail intersection between three pine thickets. I put three hen decoys and a B-Mobile gobbler decoy in the road where they were visible from all approaches. Turkeys were late to vocalize, but I was thrilled to be near at least four different gobblers. One tom flapped to the ground with a thud about one hundred yards up the hill. It had a deep, throaty gobble, and I suspected it was a bird that I had worked in 2012 and 2013. A second tom was a screamer. Working two aggressive gobblers is ideal because it creates a competitive situation in which they often race to reach a hen call first. If they followed that script, they would come into this little hollow to gobble and strut. There they would find the decoys, and one would earn a ride out of the woods on my shoulder.

Instead, all the gobblers went the other direction, but the fuse was lit for the defining campaign of my budding turkey hunting career. I knew I had a legitimate chance with at least two gobblers, but I soon became obsessed with killing the one I nicknamed "The Boss." He was the alpha gobbler that ruled these woods, and he was the one that continually picked up my gauntlet. The Boss was my most worthy opponent to date, and I was determined to prove myself equally worthy.

On April 21, I went to the same area. The screamer closed fast from an unexpected direction and hung up out of sight before leaving the way it came. Before the hunt ended, I saw two strutters in an open spot that was unapproachable in daylight, but I intended to occupy that position at dawn.

The next morning, I arrived in the dark and placed the hen decoys near the spot where I saw the strutters. At about 8 a.m., The Boss announced his arrival. It was the tom with the deep, cello-toned gobble. He was in range, but he was invisible and safe among thick brush. I purred and clucked with my diaphragm. The Boss bellowed in response. Preparation was about to meet opportunity.

The Boss had other ideas. He veered north and stayed in the pines, gobbling salty retorts to the taunts of a crow that claimed the same territory. He proceeded into a wooded draw, and I could hear his encounter with a hen about twenty minutes later. A spirited commotion accompanied that tryst, and The Boss continued into the heart of the pine thicket, not to return.

After taking a break on April 22, I was sure I had The Boss patterned on April 23. I set up without decoys before sunrise in a clump of brush at the edge of a draw. I wore a ghillie poncho, face net, and gloves. Dawn was quiet, but I heard clucks around 7:30 a.m. Then, I saw shapes bobbing through a screen of brush. They were probably hens, but I raised my gun in case a gobbler trailed them. The girls were enjoying a casual morning stroll through the neighborhood. They clucked and purred all the latest woodland gossip, but they froze when they saw the ghillie-covered mass. They were twelve feet away, indecisive but curious.

"Oh, my, what is that ugly thing?" Purr, cluck! Purr, cluck!

"I don't know, but it doesn't look like it wants to eat us!" Purr, cluck!

With no gobbler near, I lowered the shotgun. The movement provoked a cacophony of cackles. One hen ran into the fringe of the woods, and the other flew up to a low tree branch. It was too small to bear the hen's weight, so she lurched, bounced, and swayed like a drugstore cowgirl on a mechanical bull. Flapping and cackling, she provoked a furious response from The Boss, who listened from his strutting zone atop the hill.

The hens purred and clucked loudly, and I mocked them. They cutt and cackled, and I mocked them louder. That really aggravated them, and the trash talk excited The Boss. The hens were anxious to go to him. Unfortunately for me, he was not anxious to come to them. The first hen reemerged from the woods, and the other hen flapped out of the tree. I couldn't allow them to unite, so I flapped my arms. That turned the hens back away from The Boss, but it also infuriated them. They cutt and cackled, and I returned every retort.

The Boss thundered from the woods, but instead of showing himself, he retreated deeper into cover. The overwrought hens fretted loudly over their departing paramour, but their clamoring summoned a two-year-old gobbler from the dark shadows of the pines. He was in range, but I didn't dare shoot that bird with The Boss so close. If I did, I would probably never see or hear The Boss again.

About fifteen minutes later, a third hen joined the first two. They massed at the edge of the trail and flew across, cackling maniacally like teenyboppers rushing the stage at a Justin Bieber concert. I met those hens again at about 5:30 p.m., at a different spot. The Boss was not with them. He was more of a morning socializer, but I knew where to meet him for breakfast.

Work kept me away until April 26, when I slipped well before dawn into the middle of The Boss's strutting parlor. It was a small opening among the pines. The Boss went there daily to gobble and preen before easing through the thicket and crossing a road into a small hollow. On that morning, however, he entered the parlor from a different direction than usual. I was hamstrung because he was too close. I hoped he would walk past me and get in front, but instead he stood behind and stared at my back for fifteen minutes. I must have twitched from a mosquito bite because The Boss putted and flew away.

Those Grant County piney woods birds are the flightiest turkeys I've ever seen. Turkeys usually run from trouble. These birds fly at the slightest provocation, I guess because the forest floor is too littered and tangled to run efficiently.

That encounter tattered my nerves. The Boss and I needed a timeout, so I stayed away for four days to regroup and strategize. I hoped that my long absence would give him time to calm down as well.

In my favor was the fact that I hadn't actually bumped The Boss. The flyaway incident was merely a response to movement, but I was certain he didn't actually see me. That meant The Boss and his parlor were still in play. We would start fresh on April 30, but there was no margin of error. The game would be won or lost on that day, and the odds were squarely in his favor.

To that point, I had hunted in the ghillie poncho, but I was certain The Boss had linked my calls to the indistinct form of the ghillie from his vantage point in the brush. I needed to remove that image from the equation. My trusty pop-up blind was the solution.

At 5 a.m., I hauled my gear about three quarters of a mile up a dirt road on a game cart. The cart made a timorous clatter in the predawn stillness, but that wasn't the worst of it. The joints in the blind make loud thumps when they pop into place, and the fabric swishes and scrapes. I crashed around in The Boss's strutting parlor, huffing and puffing and making a terrible racket trying to untangle the spiny little hut.

Once inside, I sat down and assessed my position in the gathering light. I could not have been in a worse place. A wall of tall ferns and grass blocked my vision. Though it was well past fly-down time, I had no choice but to move the blind about forty yards to a logging road.

Unlike previous days, I heard no gobbles and no hens. All my calls were safely zipped inside my vest except for the diaphragm call in my mouth, but I remained silent. At 6:35 a.m., a hen on the logging road ran past the blind and took flight when she drew even with the front window. Wondering if the blind spooked her, I peered through the open flap to the right and saw a gobbler running up the road in the hen's wake. With a lumbering, swaying gait, he closed so fast that I barely had time to raise my shotgun. Seeing the movement, the gobbler slowed to a fast walk. His long, thick beard swung back and forth like a Croix de Guerre. It was The Boss, in range and utterly exposed.

The Boss paused tentatively as he processed the movement and the unusual presence of the blind, but his lust for the hen was too strong. He took a few more faltering steps toward me, stopped, and turned broadside toward heavy cover. He was about to bolt. I quickly ran down a mental checklist and noticed that my head was canted to the left of my gun barrel. I was looking past the left side of the green sight bead at the muzzle.

You'll miss The Boss doing that, Hoss, I thought.

I corrected my aim, squeezed the trigger, and sent two ounces of 5-6-7 Hevi Shot downrange. At 25 paces, The Boss went down like a sack of rocks. I tumbled out of the blind in case I needed a follow-up shot, but the first one was final.

The Boss had a ten-inch beard and ¾-inch spurs. I didn't weigh him, but I estimated him at about eighteen pounds. He was a dandy gobbler, especially for piney woods, taken on a day when neither the turkeys nor I made a sound.

The Boss encapsulated the inherent contradictions of turkey hunting. On the days when I did everything right, every round with The Boss ended in a draw. When I finally made what should have been a season-ending error, The Boss made a decisive error. It was only one campaign, but I felt like my luck had finally changed.

CHAPTER FOURTEEN

SOUL MATES

A competitive handgunner, Allan Griffin was also an aspiring turkey hunter who entrusted his development to my nascent abilities.

Our first outings were at Galla Creek Wildlife Management Area near Russellville, Arkansas, where we both drew permits for the same controlled-access turkey hunt. Reserved, quiet, and analytical, Griffin was a tech support representative for a regional wireless communications service provider. Tall and slight, he wore eyeglasses that, along with his receding wisp of red hair, gave him a professorial demeanor. He sang in his church choir and was occasionally a featured soloist. His life was an orderly devotion to process. He asked a lot of questions, and he listened with an attentiveness so intense that he sometimes came off as critical.

Those attributes made Griffin a natural fit for competitive handgunning. There is a correct methodology to advance through a tactical handgun course. You get points for doing it right and points deducted for doing it wrong. It is orderly and doctrinal, which puts it diametrically out of phase with turkey hunting. As much as Griffin tried to embrace it, the improvisational nature of turkey hunting—and especially that of his mentor—mystified him.

During our Galla Creek hunt, we camped at Sweeden Island, a now-closed public campground on a high bank overlooking the Arkansas River. We pitched our tents at the edge of a bluff and retired early. At about 2 a.m., I sat bolt upright in my sleeping bag. The inside of my tent was ablaze with brilliant white light overlain by a throbbing hum. I shook off my slumber and emerged from my tent to find a bewildered Griffin standing in boxer shorts beside his tent. A towboat churning upstream toward Dardanelle Lock & Dam used its spotlight to search for red and green navigational markers. The pilot trained the spotlight on us. I reciprocated by dropping my shorts and presenting my backside.

"Moon's low tonight, Cap'n," I grumbled.

Griffin's jaw dropped wordlessly, but the incident was not mentioned again.

We struck a gobbler shortly after dawn. It was very close.

"Don't worry about me," I said. "This is your bird. I'll call him in for you. When he's in range, I'll make a loud putt. When he raises his head, shoot him."

We never saw the gobbler, but the close call enraptured Griffin. We spent the afternoon hunting a fallow sunflower field where I had seen turkeys in the past, but none appeared. At the end of the hot and windy day, we solaced ourselves with a hot meal in Russellville.

That was the night Griffin met Alan Thomas, a close friend and accomplice in scores of hunting and fishing trips. Thomas, loud and bawdy with a raucous laugh and an acid wit, makes a lifestyle of ribald chaos.

As we approached our campsite, Griffin's headlights illuminated Thomas sitting on the tailgate of my pickup truck. His left hand held a beer bottle. His right arm was draped around my turkey decoy. His truck's stereo blared Dwight Yoakam's CD *Second Hand Heart*.

Thomas and I greeted each other with a hearty bear hug followed by catch-up conversation at a machine-gun pace that kept Griffin's head bobbing.

"Where'd you eat?" Thomas asked.

"Some burger joint," I replied.

"Butcher Boy?" Thomas asked.

"I think that's the one," I replied. "The one with the old-school drive-in vibe. We looked all over, but we couldn't find Joe's Crab Shack."

"Joe's Crab Shack? In Russellville?" Thomas asked. "There ain't one."

"No Joe's?" I asked with affected disappointment. Then, I screamed an expletive, thrusting my shoulders forward and drawing out the wail as long as my breath allowed. Thomas recoiled, eyes wide, and then erupted into hysterical laughter. Griffin fidgeted nervously at the acrid whiff of menace in the air.

Thomas relived some of the highlights of the previous duck season on Lake Dardanelle, where we often hunted together. One of our favorite boat launch sites is at Spadra Recreation Area.

It's a rare day at a boat ramp not to be accosted for idle conversation by boat ramp cruisers. The encounters are benign. Usually, the cruisers are bored elderly men driving around hoping to encounter a friend or acquaintance launching or trailering a boat. If friends aren't available, strangers suffice. Jehovah's Witnesses have preached to me on boat ramps. I've engaged in all manner of social and political discussions. I've dispensed fishing advice and had it dispensed, sometimes on request.

Boat ramp cruisers have a distinctive mien. Almost all are chain smokers who speak with tobacco-tortured growls. Their skin is leathery and spotted, often with varying degrees of melanoma, from lifetimes spent on the water without sun protection. They wear Wrangler jeans and running shoes with oversized, thickly cushioned soles. Most travel with small dogs that ride on their laps, often with their heads out the window.

The Spadra ramp is unique for its cadre of regulars that loiters at the day-use area. As Thomas stowed his gear after a hunt, one of the Spadra regulars quizzed Thomas about his morning's activities. He placed his dachshund in Thomas's boat, where the dog promptly defecated.

"What's your problem?" Thomas demanded.

"What!?" asked the man.

"Your damn dog shit in my boat!"

"Only a little bit," the man replied dismissively.

"Well, clean it the hell up!" Thomas demanded.

The man refused. Words were exchanged. Voices raised and tempers flared until Thomas scooped up the poop in his bare hand and flung it against the owner's chest.

The owner called the sheriff. A deputy responded and told the old man he was lucky he didn't get his ass beat, and if anyone deserved to go to jail, it was him.

Recounting the incident, Thomas praised the cleverness and creativity of the old man's insults, an art at which Thomas himself excels.

"He got in some pretty good zingers, but I acquitted myself well," Thomas said. "All in all, I'd call it a draw."

Soon after Thomas concluded that tale, a chatty campground host arrived, speech slurred and reeking of alcohol. Seeing beer, he invited himself into our gathering. He irritated Thomas with an odd tale of having cooked and eaten a venomous coral snake skewered on a telescoping car antenna remnant. Thomas humored his intrusion until the host declared that, as table fare, snow goose is superior to wild turkey.

"That right there proves that you're an ignorant dumbass, my friend," Thomas blurted. "Snow goose isn't worthy to even be mentioned in the same sentence as wild turkey. For you to say something that stupid proves that you've never eaten snow goose or wild turkey! You have no credibility, so please be quiet."

The interloper rose and advanced on Thomas, who rose to answer the challenge. The interloper halted, seeing that Thomas was considerably bigger than he had estimated. His tone and demeanor quickly turned conciliatory. After a face-saving delay, he excused himself, ostensibly to go check on some bit of faulty campground infrastructure.

"Go on back to your ratty-ass motor home and fry yourself up a heaping helping of nasty-ass snow goose, you coral-snake-eatin' douchebag," Thomas muttered as the interloper departed.

Griffin stood shell-shocked and awestruck. He'd read about Alan Thomas in my columns for years, but the newspaper version paled to the legend in the flesh.

In May 2014, I fulfilled a promise to take Griffin to some of my secret haunts in the Ozark Mountains after I killed a wily old bird back home that I nicknamed The Boss. As the campaign against The Boss dragged on, Griffin despaired that the season would end without his taking a mentored hunt. He rejoiced when I finally bagged The Boss. He said he had been praying precisely for that outcome, so he and the Almighty are officially credited with an assist in the box score.

A day after I fired The Boss, Griffin and I were hunting turkeys in the mountains, which required that Griffin be initiated into the Hagarville Breakfast Club.

Hagarville, population 142, is a wide spot at a crossroads in northern Johnson County. I often hunt deer nearby in the Ozark National Forest, and part of my daily deer hunting routine is to visit the Hagarville Grocery for a breakfast sandwich. It's about seven miles from my camp to the grocery, but it's a guilty pleasure that breaks the monotony of the hunt routine.

The store is old, with creaky wooden floors that amplify ambient noise and voices. In addition to staples, the store carries many basic items required for routine rural home maintenance like fuses, pipe fittings and couplings, basic electrical components, and, of course, duct tape. There's a lot of duct tape and also a small amount of fishing tackle. More complicated projects require a visit to Leonard's Hardware in Russellville or to Lowe's, which means a half-day trip and significant fuel consumption.

The grocery store is the locus for culture and entertainment in Hagarville. Sit long enough and you will gain a rudimentary knowledge of the community and its inhabitants, like the barber who complains of being penniless but whose shop never seems to be open.

"I'm open on Sunday by necessity," said Dave, the grocery store's proprietor, who makes one of the best bacon-egg-cheese toasters this side of Little Rock. "The only day I close is Christmas."

On this day, repairmen were working on a malfunctioning gasoline pump. It looked to be an easy fix. The brass gears merely needed lubricant.

"You gonna get you one of them new digital pumps?" a customer asked.

"You know how much one of those things costs?" Dave asked, scoffing. "I only make a nickel a gallon. It'd take the rest of my life to pay for one."

The customer's booming laugh reverberated through the building.

As Griffin and I ate, a local gentleman sat down at our table. He didn't offer his name and I didn't ask, nor did he ask for ours. Griffin and I wore turkey hunting clothes, and since he identified himself as a turkey hunter, he concluded that Griffin and I would welcome his company. And we did.

It's common for strangers to share a table at little places like this because there are few tables, and ours had the best view of the television. Besides, why sit alone when you can share breakfast communally?

Our anonymous friend lamented the dearth of turkeys in this part of the world. Griffin and I commiserated. In two days of hard hunting, we had not heard a gobble. We had not seen any turkey sign. We had walked many miles through the Piney Creeks Wildlife Management Area, but all we had to show for our effort was some severe sinus congestion for Griffin and some wide blisters on my heels and toes, thanks entirely to a lifelong allegiance—which I had not yet renounced—to improperly sized shoes.

Southerners of a certain age learned to size shoes the way our mothers taught us, with an unspecific amount of free space between the big toe and inside wall of the shoe, and various other imprecise, arbitrary estimates. All my life I wore size 8 ½ shoes. At age 24, I backpacked from Arkansas to Maine in size 8 ½ shoes. My feet were always sore and in disrepair. I was fifty-two years old in 2015 when a podiatrist taught me how to properly size my feet. One foot is size 10. The other is 9 ½. My width is D. More than midway through my life, I finally learned the divinity of properly fitting footwear. It turned groans to contented sighs and grouchiness to bliss. My feet haven't hurt since.

"I think predators have as much to do with it as anything," our friend said, speaking not of sore feet but of turkey deprivation. He hissed contemptuously and added, "The Game and Fish, they've told me that eighty percent of the hatch is going to be lost anyway, no matter what. Turkeys can absorb that if you have a hundred broods because you'll still have twenty percent survival, but when you get down to five broods, you've still got the same number of predators. They're gonna get every damn one of them! It's a case of diminishing returns."

Case in point, he said, was a hen he'd watched on his property.

"She started out with nine poults," he said. "A few days later she was down to seven. Then she was down to five. Eventually she was down to one, and then she didn't have any. No way you can tell me turkeys have a chance around here with all the things that are out there eating them."

On the other hand, hunters did kill sixty-eight adult gobblers in Piney Creeks Wildlife Management Area in 2014. They probably killed most of them early in the season on the accessible southern end where Griffin and I hunted. Had I planned our outing better, and had I worn properly fitting boots, we would have ventured much deeper into the interior and farther from the roads.

"The thing I love most about turkey hunting is that nothing you learned from the last hunt applies to the next hunt," I said, our friend nodding. "Anytime you hear somebody say, 'Turkeys always do this or do that,' you know that person isn't a turkey hunter because turkeys don't always do anything."

That statement melted away the last of our friend's cautious reserve.

"A turkey is nothing more than a highly sophisticated motion detector system with zero curiosity," he said. "A deer is a highly sophisticated motion detector system with a lot of curiosity. They'll come to you to see what you are. Not a turkey. If it sees movement, it's gone. No curiosity at all."

He said he was most amazed at a turkey's ability to pinpoint sound sources.

"They can hear a long ways off, and they'll fly a long ways off the roost to get to a call," he said. "I had one come in to me like that one morning. I had no idea where that bird roosted. I was alone, and just like that, there he was. It was a panic attack both ways."

I think our friend would have been happy to chat all day, but Griffin and I had to get back to our spot for the magic 11 a.m–2 p.m. window through which, unfortunately, the magician failed to appear.

A column I wrote about that morning hangs framed in the Hagarville Grocery. When I returned in the fall for a deer hunt, I introduced myself to Dave as its author, and we became instant friends.

"It was a happy coincidence that guy showed up while you were here," said Dave. "He was the perfect person for you to meet at that time. He's as big a turkey hunter as we have around here."

"I noticed he didn't invite us to hunt on his place," I said.

"No, no, that didn't surprise me one bit," Dave said, laughing. "I've known him all my life, and he's never invited me either."

CHAPTER FIFTEEN

THE LUMBERJACK

M any of my great turkey hunts have started reluctantly and with a seemingly disastrous mental lapse. So consistent are these two elements not just in turkey hunting but in all sectors of my life, that I recognize them as providential.

April 12, 2017, the third day of Arkansas's spring turkey season, began with such a lapse. It was 3:30 a.m., and I could not rouse myself from bed. A sore throat and low fever knocked out Tuesday's hunt, and I was still piqued over an uneventful hunt on Monday's opener April 10.

Nothing's going to happen this morning, anyway, I thought as I looked at the clock. *I'll sleep in and hunt this afternoon.*

I was still wide-awake at 4:30 a.m., mind roiling with questions, answers, and questions to answers. My fidgeting irritated my wife, so I prodded myself upright, brewed a Thermos full of coffee, and trudged out to the truck. The sky was clear, and the air was cool and calm.

If they're going to gobble, it'll be on a morning like this, I thought.

Reaching my intended hunting spot in thirty minutes required driving a certain route through backroads in Hot Spring and Saline counties. I started the truck, turned on Sirius XM, and jotted my mileage and the purpose of my trip in my logbook. A quick tour through my favorite channels revealed nothing I wanted to hear. I really wanted silence, so I turned off the radio and quickly detoured through the meandering side streets and back alleys of introspection. When I snapped back to attention, I was on I-30 headed to Little Rock, about eighteen miles north of my destination and too many miles off course to backtrack. I would have to exit the interstate at Benton, wind through town, and take a two-lane highway south. If all the traffic lights were green, I would lose about twenty precious minutes.

I was momentarily angry, but I accepted the possibility that the lapse was one of those "God" things that sometimes welds us to destiny. Throughout my life, I've often heeded inexplicable internal nudges to leave a place early or take an unusual route and discover later that doing so had likely spared me from calamity.

An example was opening day of the 2019 Arkansas dove season. My broadcast partner Ray Tucker and I joined professional bass fishermen George Cochran and Larry Nixon for Cochran's annual cleanup at Bayou Meto Wildlife Management Area (WMA), a world-famous duck hunting hotspot in southeast Arkansas. Cochran owns a cabin adjacent to the WMA, and for many years he has organized a popular cleanup event that always concludes with a fish fry.

After the volunteers departed from the 2019 event, Tucker, Cochran, Nixon, and I spent the night at Cochran's cabin, watching college football and swapping stories. I'm an occasional imbiber, and that night was one of those occasions. I overindulged and drydocked myself for the morning's dove hunt, which, because of how the calendar fell, had the rare distinction of starting on a Sunday. My dove hunting host sent me a text message at about 5 a.m., asking if I were coming.

"No," I replied after chasing the phone around the nightstand with a sluggish hand. "Hungover."

"LOL!" he replied.

Later that day, I learned state and federal game wardens raided my friend's dove field and cited him for illegal baiting. In this case, "baiting" meant a small amount of corn deposited or spilled in a turnrow, but such is the nebulous netherworld of migratory bird hunting regulations. Merely being present would have been embarrassing, professionally compromising, and potentially expensive. It would also have raged like a crown fire over the internet. Message board trolls would have had a defamatory festival. It is the only instance I can recall when liquor actually kept somebody out of trouble.

A similar incident happened when I was in college. My group of friends got way too rowdy at a public campground on the Arkansas River near Little Rock. With the party winding down, I wandered to the riverside to recompose myself. When I finally returned, my friends were all gone, but their cars were still there. In my absence, the police came and hauled everyone off to jail.

A few hours later, I reported to work at John Barleycorn's Vision, a famous west Little Rock establishment in the 1970s and early '80s. The upper floor was a bar that featured live music from young acts on the rise or veteran acts in the descending arcs of their careers. One of the latter was Sam & Dave, a soul and R&B duo popular in the 1960s. They played at Barleycorn's on a Saturday night in 1981, the last year they toured together.

I was too young to be in the bar, but I had accrued stealth bar privileges during my long tenure. I amassed them gradually by carrying dirty glasses from the bar to the dishwasher downstairs, and carrying clean glasses, ice, carbonation tanks, soda syrup, and flatware up to the bar. I brought food up from the kitchen and ran other errands. The bar staff came to rely on me and was too busy to notice when I lingered by the stairwell door to savor the sights and sounds.

With the bar closed for Sam & Dave's afternoon sound check, I took a seat in front of the stage. Besides the two bartenders, the only people in the bar were Sam and Dave, their band, sound technician, and lighting crew. I sat close enough to touch the two aging stars.

With sweat cascading down their cheeks and brows, their neck muscles were as taut as braided cable as they tore through "Soul Man," "Hold On, I'm Comin'," and "When Something Is Wrong With My Baby."

Only a dozen or so people were in the room, but it may as well have been 10,000 as far as they were concerned. They poured their hearts into that sound check and then gave even more for the actual performance that evening. That was a life lesson for me. Now matter how small the gig, give it your best.

The lower floor was a restaurant that was famous for its themed sections. One room was a bank. One was a World War I bunker. Another was a circus tent where I had the honor of serving Evel Knievel, a hero to many men of my generation. I was a junior in high school the night he arrived in the company of a young woman with a theatrically disproportionate topside and a sculpted mane of platinum-colored hair held aloft by an entire can of hairspray. Her white cocktail dress was so tight that it appeared to have been applied with an airbrush. She and Knievel were as red as lobsters, and he could barely sit upright without assistance. He scrawled a Rorschach blot of an autograph on a cocktail napkin and pushed it toward me through a puddle of condensation. There was no distinction between the man and his caricature, and it all seemed so perfectly appropriate.

In 1995, when I was a reporter for the *Southwest Times-Record* in Fort Smith, Arkansas, a tipster called the sports department.

"Hey," he said. "Wanna see Evel Knievel's rocket bike?"

In 1974, Knievel attempted to jump a mile-wide chasm across Idaho's Snake River Canyon with a rocket-powered bike, the Skycycle X-2. The ill-fated exploit was the stuntman's high-water mark, but it was also the beginning of his descent into self-parody. The stunt failed spectacularly, but that fact has been lost in the legend. The Skycycle X-2 was in a warehouse in downtown Fort Smith as part of a restoration process as I recall. Being in its presence closed the loop that leads us back to the campground tequila fiasco, which ultimately nudges us awake in 2017, midway through our wayward route back to the turkey woods.

The morning after the campground fiasco, our manager assigned me to clean up a mess in the service bar's reach-in cooler. This was the gritty side of working in a glamorous place. The service bartender had dropped a glass of wine into the cooler the night before, and I had to remove all the shards and wine and deodorize the compartment. I stuck my head into the cooler, a large refrigerator with racks inside and a door on top, and I quickly succumbed to wine fumes that summoned forth the spirits that had not yet been exorcised from my veins. The manager, who forty years later remains a fishing buddy, prepared an elixir of tonic water and bitters and dismissed me to cut lemon wedges in hopes that the fresh citrus fumes would restore some capacity for productivity.

It was hopeless. I called a coworker who had been at the campground party. That's when I learned what happened to him and the rest of my mates. He had just arrived home after being bailed out of jail.

"Dave, I hate to do this to you, brother, but you've got to come in this morning," I said. "I'm too hung over to work."

"Man? Shit!" he wailed, drawing out the "i" with the entire breath. To his credit, he relieved me even though he was in worse shape than I was.

There are too many other examples of serendipitous misdirection to mention, but their memories reinforced my belief that my errant route to the turkey woods was preordained. Instead of griping about it, I contemplated how to play the hand I ham-handedly dealt myself.

On opening day, April 10, sitting in the same spot where a gobbler had eluded me on opening morning of the 2013 spring season, a tom gobbled once shortly after fly-down. A nearby logging crew prompted that turkey to seek quick refuge in thick woods. That was the last turkey sound I heard until about 4:15 p.m., when a tom with the same voice gobbled three times while returning quickly to its roost area overlooking the logging deck where the crew parked its equipment for the night.

There were a lot of radical variables in that equation. There was no way to know how a gobbler roosting over an industrial site would respond to a crew of noisy loggers in the morning. Any number of things could happen to make the gobbler fly, run, or walk any direction after leaving the roost. If hens were nearby, the loggers could influence how they left the roost too. Wherever the hens went, the gobbler would stay close to them.

It was all immaterial on April 12 because my errant route prohibited me from reaching that spot on time. Instead, it led me to my favorite deer hunting spot on the other side of the logging site, about a half-mile away. At that time, it was the prettiest section of woods in that part of the Old Belfast Hunting Club. Great thickets bordered two sides. A young cutover bordered another side, and a four-year-old cutover bordered a fourth side. Food and cover were abundant, and there were open areas for a gobbler to strut and display.

It was already light when I arrived, so I placed two hen decoys conspicuously in a firebreak, a move that nearly proved regrettable. I put on my ghillie poncho and gloves. I unpacked a collection of calls that included an Eddie Horton box made of black walnut with a bloodwood lid, a Bill Rhodes chinaberry box, and a small chinaberry slate call made by David Taylor of Sheridan, along with a David Taylor custom striker. I also mouthed a Premium Game Calls diaphragm. It's easy to blow, and its raspy tone resonates in thick woods.

At about 6:40 a.m., I started scratching the Taylor slate. Its high, sweet tone is loud but not overbearing, and it carries well in piney woods. From nearly a quarter of a mile away, up near the logging area, the chuckle of a distant gobble pricked my ear through the din of rattling chains, the hollow thumps of hydraulic fluid jugs being thrown about, and the slamming of engine cowlings. The Lumberjack had reported for work.

That was the first time I ever played Horton's walnut box in the woods, and the opening note made my heart leap. It was rich and clear, with a subtle rasp and a finishing bite. At a distance, it had to have sounded like a real hen. I scratched out a few plaintive yelps and then countered with a yelping sequence on the diaphragm. Another gobble crackled through the pines a few minutes later. It was louder and closer.

A "search" gobble has a distinct, interrogative timbre. The gobbler is looking for the ersatz hen, but this is a dangerous time because it's also when a real hen is most likely to pick off a questing gobbler. If that happens in turkey-rich states, you have the option of repositioning and trying to find another gobbler. In Arkansas, the one gobbler you hear at dawn is probably the only gobbler you will hear all day. If you miss at dawn, your only option is to try to call the tom back at noon after he and the hen have separated.

From closer still came a third search gobble. I made one more series of yelps on the box and then followed with a burst of clucks. I finished with a long series of purrs on the slate.

The next gobble sounded different. It was assertive, and its source was coming fast. This is a critical moment when you can easily err. Should I be quiet, aggressive, or somewhere in between? I chose the latter. I clucked and purred with all three calls, with an occasional yelp on the slate.

Moments later came the most beautiful, most awe-inspiring sight of my hunting career. Facing the sunrise, I looked down a straight row of tall pines that split the light into two towering shafts that swirled like molten crystal in the mist. Through my persimmon-tinted shades, the effect was ethereal, like stained glass. I had seen hints of it in deer season, but at that moment the place exuded a holiness akin to that of a church, and the glory of creation was in full display in the apse that would endure in my soul as St. Tom's Cathedral.

At the top of the rise, about 150 yards away in the middle of a firebreak, the brown tips of The Lumberjack's outstretched fan glowed like a fiery halo backlit by the sunrise. The Lumberjack stopped, struck a rock star pose, threw out his neck, and belted out a loud, cackling gobble. Then he retracted his neck, spun, pranced, and swayed down the illuminated firebreak like a fashion model on a runway. He took three or four steps, spun his fan around like a radar dish, tilting it to the left and to the right. He dragged his wingtips as he strutted, throwing up pine needles in his wake. He zigged a few steps to the right, spun his fan, and then zagged a few steps to the left.

Heart racing and hyperventilating, I pushed my diaphragm around my suddenly dry mouth with my tongue and mustered up enough saliva to purr. The Lumberjack lowered his feathers, trotted ten to fifteen yards and then displayed again. He thrust out his neck and bellowed an entirely different kind of gobble. It was deep and resonant, booming basso and bluster. He lusted for sex, and he demanded that the hen come out from hiding and give it to him.

He continued his triumphal march. Sixty yards. Fifty. Forty-five. Forty. The gobbler grew larger and grander with each step, marching straight to my lair without the merest threat of straying.

Inside my Winchester SX3 was a trio of three-inch, Winchester Long Beard Extra Range shells packed with 1 ⅞ ounces of No. 6 shot. They threw a lethal pattern to sixty yards through a Trulock .660 constriction extended choke tube. I also zeroed a Truglo fiber optic site to forty yards, but I would not shoot until necessary. I wanted this ballet to last.

I waited for The Lumberjack to top the rise, but the ruse nearly imploded when he finally saw the decoys. I have noticed that two or more gobblers together will mingle with decoys. A single gobbler with no competition expects hens to follow him, so he will often display at a distance and then veer away. The Lumberjack did precisely that. Shielded by a tree, he stopped and eyed the inert hens suspiciously. He intended to turn back downhill and drift into a thicket on a path that offered no clear shot.

I blew a cackle on the diaphragm, followed by a fighting purr on a pair of finger friction calls that I use for that purpose only. The Lumberjack displayed, then pivoted and walked about three yards into the open toward the decoys. He stopped, pulled in his feathers and stood straight.

At nineteen yards, the mass of the load slammed The Lumberjack like a cornerback leveling an outstretched receiver. The gobbler fell out of sight below the rise and did not flop. I sat with my gun trained on the spot where I last saw him for about thirty seconds. Seeing no movement, I rose and advanced slowly with my gun at port arms, poised to snap shoot like I would on a flushing pheasant. I was almost upon the gobbler when I finally saw him, dead.

The shot-buffering material coated his feathers like talcum powder. His beard was 9 ¾ inches long, and his spurs were three-quarters of an inch long. He weighed about eighteen pounds. The time was 7:10 a.m., about the time my daughters would have been boarding the school bus at home. I wished them as fine a day as mine, and then I registered my kill as required on the Arkansas Game and Fish Commission's online app.

Wood finches and nuthatches flitted among the trees as the morning mist continued to swirl in the light. I sat against a pine tree and admired my gobbler as I imprinted every minute of this tango to memory. It was a form of worship that included a profoundly heartfelt prayer of thanksgiving, not just for the gobbler but also for the health, desire, and good fortune to partake in the moment.

It was a long walk back to the truck with the gobbler's bony legs pressing into my shoulder and its spurs pressing into my hands. Its outstretched tail bounced back and forth with every step, filling my nose with a musky bouquet of turkey scent. I went slowly, basking in the sweet song of the woodland choir, my body and soul throbbing with the pulsing warmth of contentment. It was the finest church service of my life.

Chapter Sixteen

THE MADISON DOCTRINE

Hunting turkeys on private land is hard enough. Hunting them on public land is harder, invoking a separate set of complicating variables that tax the limits of one's skill and patience.

If you regularly hunt the same private acreages, you learn where turkeys roost, where they loaf and dust, where they retire in the afternoons, and, most importantly, where other hunters go and don't go.

On public land, other hunters comprise a radical factor that skews every other variable. Human traffic not only influences turkey movements and behavior, but it also increases the likelihood that another hunter will bump or intercept a gobbler that you are working. Finding birds that you can pattern on public ground requires getting away from roads and searching inaccessible corners that other people are disinclined to visit. The only way to ensure privacy is also to find a place so remote that nobody else can hear turkeys gobble.

Because of the work and luck involved, successfully hunting gobblers on public land is a major accomplishment, but that's only one reason why President Madison means so much to me. He was my first Ozarks gobbler and also my first mountain gobbler.

Madison County Wildlife Management Area (WMA) sprawls across 14,536 acres of steep, rugged country in the heart of the Ozark Mountains between the Arkansas towns of Huntsville and Eureka Springs. Its knobby hills aren't very high, but its hollows are very deep. Loose limestone and sandstone chert cover nearly every acre, just waiting to roll an ankle or wrench a knee.

Two noncontiguous units compose the WMA. The south unit terrain is a bit gentler and contains a lot of fields that were planted to provide food for deer before the Arkansas Game and Fish Commission detected chronic wasting disease in Madison County in 2016. Chronic wasting disease is a fatal neurological disease that is specific to deer, elk, and moose. Concentrating deer is believed to facilitate transmission, so the Game and Fish Commission curtailed the use of food plots on public land within its chronic wasting disease management zones. Of course, turkeys use food plots too. Discontinuing them at Madison County WMA also discourages turkey concentrations and contributes to their dispersal.

As a whole, Madison County WMA is forested with oak and hickory, but it has some small pine groves and cedar thickets. Thanks to the Ozark region's karst topography, the WMA also has an abundance of natural springs that pour through openings in the limestone bluffs, creating beautiful sightseeing destinations and photographic opportunities. In a wet spring, people from nearby cities such as Fayetteville, Springdale, Rogers, and Bentonville flock to the WMA to search for waterfalls. For turkey hunters, waterfall hunters are yet another variable that can influence success.

Turkey hunting is allowed at Madison County WMA for only six days in the form of two controlled-access hunts that take place on the first and second weekends of the 16-day spring turkey season. In 2016, the hunts occurred April 16–18 and April 23–25. I was very fortunate to have obtained permits for both hunts, which I got through stubborn perseverance. The Arkansas Game and Fish Commission awards controlled hunt permits through a computerized lottery, but some winners don't claim their permits. If you're lucky, you can buy an unclaimed permit in a first-come, first-served online sale ten days after the drawing.

The unclaimed permit sale begins on a Monday at 8 a.m. Thousands of hopeful applicants hover over their keyboards waiting for the sale to go live. For several years, the system crashed from the avalanche of logins, and it took hours for the agency's program vendor to reboot the system. Most hopefuls didn't have the time or patience to continually refresh the purchase page, so they abandoned their vigils and got on with their business. I was persistent and got permits for both hunts. I needed the second permit because of what happened in the first hunt.

I arrived on a sunny afternoon and made camp in one of the WMA's many remote campgrounds, which are merely mowed openings with no amenities. I pitched my tent beneath a big oak tree, arranged my bedding, and erected a long table for my propane camp stove, water, and utensils. While I set up camp, a local resident driving around the area stopped to visit. He warned me about the madhouse I would encounter in the morning. Hunters would swarm the WMA, he said, and most of them would sit on the roadsides listening for gobblers. If I worked a gobbler, I'd better close the deal quickly because somebody would cut in front of me and intercept the turkey or scare it away, he said.

It wasn't that way at all. A lot of people drove through that area at dawn the next morning, but I was the only person who actually hunted in that entire sector. More accurately, I was the only person who hunted legally in that sector. Three men camped in the same opening where I did. They were vague and evasive about sharing where they planned to hunt, which I asked only to avoid encroaching on them and to dissuade them from encroaching on me.

Another complicating factor was having to cover weigh-ins for a major bass tournament at Beaver Lake, which coincided precisely with my hunt. That meant I had to stop hunting at about 1 p.m., return to camp to bathe, wash my hair, and shave, and then drive about one hour across the mountains to reach the venue near Rogers before the weigh-ins began. After each weigh-in, I went to a coffee shop in Rogers that had free Wi-Fi and filed my stories with the newspaper. I didn't return to camp until very late.

At the end of the first day, my evasive neighbors had struck camp when I returned, but they left a turkey feather in my tent rigging. It turned out that they didn't have a permit to hunt and had poached a gobbler off private land adjacent to the wildlife management area that just happened to be owned by Bobby Wilson, the area's manager. Wilson was very interested in hosting a meeting between them and the game warden. I shared the details that I remembered, and I heard that the interlopers were caught and cited for numerous violations.

April nights in the Ozarks are cool and windy on the ridgetops. My supper on the eve of my first hunt was thinly sliced beef rib eye and shrimp, stir-fried in extra-virgin olive oil with sliced red, green, and yellow peppers, mushrooms, asparagus tips, and finely diced garlic and onion. Extra-virgin is a curious description. I am not aware that there are degrees of virginity. Dicing the garlic and onions was laborious, but I savored the effort anticipating the reward. In a cast-iron skillet on a Coleman stove, I sautéed the aggregation while adding ground Himalayan pink salt and lemon pepper. The steamy aroma swaddled my senses like a mother's embrace. I could have eaten it straight from the skillet, but to maintain a degree of civility, I took my servings from an enameled steel plate while sipping a good pinot noir.

After supper, I pulled up a chair beside a roaring campfire and relaxed with a single shot of fine neat bourbon. I was mellow and content, and I slept soundly under the rustling leaves of the oak.

On the first Saturday, I hunted in a deep hollow where I encountered an ancient gobbler with a gimpy leg while hunting deer the previous autumn. I did not expect or even hope to encounter the same gobbler seven months later, but that turkey was in a natural travel funnel that connects the WMA with private land. It is a good place to waylay birds moving to or from the fields in the afternoon.

Hunting that area was a big mistake. To the disservice of hunters and nonhunters, the Game and Fish Commission does not restrict nonhunters from its WMAs during controlled-access hunts, nor does it post notices that say controlled hunts are in progress. As I prepared to enter the woods, a young family from Bentonville arrived in a stylish, late-model crossover vehicle to search for waterfalls. The adults and their two children wore clothing colored with generous amounts of red, white, and blue, the colors of an aroused gobbler's head during mating season. Wearing those colors creates an opportunity to be mistaken for a turkey and unwittingly invites a hunting accident.

Bentonville, the headquarters for Walmart, attracts employees from all over the world. Many are young representatives attached to Walmart's vendors. Several big trucking companies based in the area also attract a diverse workforce from outside of Arkansas. Tyson Foods, another worldwide enterprise, is based in nearby Springdale and likewise employs people from around the globe. Many, if not most, are nonhunters from nonhunting communities or backgrounds.

My shotgun was cased in the truck while I chatted amiably with the couple. I mentioned that a controlled turkey hunt was in progress, and while the risk of an adverse encounter was very low, their attire was probably not appropriate at that time.

"You mean, people are hunting out here? Right now?" asked the father, his voice rising an octave.

"Uh, yeah. That's why I'm here," I said. "You know, the camo and all? Like I said, the risk is very low, and we're all very careful, but you might want to rethink your color schemes."

"Should we leave? How long does this hunt last?" asked the father.

"You don't need to leave on my account," I replied. "Yours is the only car here, and there aren't any vehicles on the road between here and my campsite, so nobody else is in the woods from this direction. But somebody might have come in from one of the roads on the other side of the mountain. There are trails with signs leading to the best waterfalls. Hunters know where those are and generally stay away from them, so it's all good except for the colors."

"What about you?" asked the father.

"I was going where you're going, but I'm going to leave you to it," I replied. "I'll go somewhere else well away from here. Have fun and be careful."

Reassured, they thanked me for the advice and, still clad in red, white, and blue, they trod single file down the trail into the hollow where I had intended to go. That forced me to recalibrate and find a place that was unlikely to attract sightseers and hikers. Unfortunately, that might also force other hunters to seek the same places, so I would have to work extra hard to find a place to myself.

I found it in a remote part of the area where I've often hunted deer. Getting there required walking about three-quarters of a mile.

On the second day of the hunt, I sat near the top of a rise over-looking a short, narrow mountain bench that interrupts the hill's nearly vertical, 200-yard descent into a hollow. Above that bench is a shorter, narrower bench where I placed two decoys. Covered in my ghillie poncho, I sat in a ground chair beside a fallen tree among a tangle of branches where I had a clear, 150-degree field of view.

No gobblers answered my call, but an hour later, a hen walked up the draw behind me. I was surprised at how noisy she was. She continued down the hill to the bench below and ducked into her nest in a briar thicket. I flushed her off the nest when I departed, but we were frequent companions for the next two days. She came out in the mornings to eat, returned to her nest for most of the day, and probably came back out for supper in the late afternoon.

I woke to cold rain Monday, the final day of the hunt. I intended to go home, but the hard rain abated to a light drizzle about the time I reached my usual parking spot. I'd come too far not to play the final quarter, so I gathered my gear for one last walk across the ridge. I set up at the same latitude, but I moved to the base of two giant trees that gave me a full view of the most likely approaches.

Shortly after, a turkey entered the clearing below. I called, and it came right to me. It was the nesting hen. She sidled up to one decoy and fluffed up her feathers. She purred aggressively and acted as if she might attack the decoy. Instead, she hopped to one side and shook water all over it.

I guess she told you! I thought, amused.

About an hour later, a different turkey answered my call with deep, raspy clucks, like those of a guinea fowl. They came from a direction I didn't expect, and the tree that served as my back-rest obscured my view. The clucks reverberated in the still, cool air.

When the turkey entered the clearing, the clucks became quieter and more plaintive. Then, they stopped. Minutes later, a hen appeared to my right. She saw me, reversed course, and clucked all the way back down the hill.

About ninety minutes later, a gobbler came in hot from the same direction. I assume it mated with the hen and was now lusting for a second tryst. I clucked softly and purred twice. The tom gobbled three times and went quiet. I shouldered my shotgun and waited for him to crest the knob. I held that pose for nearly fifty minutes. When I couldn't hold it any longer, I made the most elemental mistake in turkey hunting. I quit.

When I stood, a big gobbler flushed out of a blackberry bramble sixty yards away where it had settled in to rest. It flew across the hollow in apparent slow motion. This was a first, and I was highly displeased. Frustrated and disgusted, I took a break and visited Bobby Wilson, the WMA's manager, whose farm is adjacent to the WMA.

"When a bird hangs up just out of sight for an hour and a half, what in the Sam Hill is he doing?" I asked.

"He probably smells a little mouse," Wilson said with a subtle chuckle. "He's just out there taking his time and checking things out. That's probably a very old bird, and he's old for a reason. I've waited like that until noon sometimes. Those are the most rewarding birds because they're the hardest to kill."

"Did I blow my chances after bumping him like that?" I asked.

"There's probably more than one tom in there, so he's got competition for hens," Wilson said. "He didn't see you. He just saw movement, so he'll be back."

Evidently, I had found the gobbler's sunning spot where he went to chill after getting his morning satisfaction. The spot also gave a gobbler a clear view of any hens that might come onto the bench from the hollow. He might even have been watching over the hen that was nesting down the hill.

I ended the first controlled hunt a few hours early to minimize my presence on the hill, but I knew exactly where to go the next weekend. My second controlled hunt permit was like forcing overtime in a football playoff and winning the coin toss. A field goal would be useless, however. The game was sudden death, and it would take a touchdown to win it.

Ninety degrees to the right of where I hunted, the ridge tapers gently into a deep hollow from where the rat-smelling gobbler approached the previous Monday. That slope is an easy route for turkeys to travel in and out of the hollow. At the edge of the thick woods is a giant pine tree with a blackberry bramble that curls around the back like a horseshoe. I could sit against that tree and have a clear view of the hillside, and the bramble would shield me from behind and from the sides. A turkey would only see me if it walked in front of me, and then it would be very close.

As with the blue barrel in Oklahoma, I was certain I would kill a bird in that spot. I envisioned exactly how it would all go down. There was no need for additional scouting or even to conceive a back-up plan. I was going to win this game with one play.

I walked back to the truck and returned to the tree with a pop-up blind. I removed it from its bag and changed my mind. I wouldn't need it. I lugged it back to the truck and returned with my stealth chair. As I placed the chair against the tree, I noticed a little bag of anchor stakes that fell from the blind bag. It was providential, like a sign saying, "You may wander, but all roads lead back to here."

I had no doubt. This was my magic tree.

I left my backpack, decoys, and ghillie poncho in the chair against the base of the tree so I wouldn't have to carry them in the morning, but mostly I did it to prevent me from changing my mind.

Back at camp, I whipped up my signature camp-stove stir-fry. I washed it down with a cold Lagunitas India Pale Ale. I cleansed my dishes and did the rest of my nightly camp chores slowly, savoring every moment of my final night on the ridge. I took a long walk in the dark on the road beside my camp and then relaxed by the fire before plunging into a deep, contented sleep while coyotes yipped and wailed from the hollow below.

Next morning, I brewed myself a big cup of coffee, drove to my parking spot, and shouldered my shotgun, a Remington 12-gauge, V3 autoloader. As I began the long walk to my tree, I reached into my pocket to hit the lock button on my key fob. Instead, I accidentally pressed the "panic" button. All of the lights on my pickup flashed, and the horn fired off four blasts before I wrestled out my keys that had splayed across the pocket interior like a treble hook. Every turkey in Madison County must have gobbled, including several from the direction of my pine tree. I excoriated myself for that bonehead play, but it was only the equivalent of an illegal procedure penalty. It cost me five yards. It was first-and-fifteen instead of first-and-ten. No sweat. I'd get it all back with one pass.

"Chill out, and work your game plan," I mumbled.

The ground in front of the pine tree was so hard that I bent a decoy stake trying to pound it with a rock. Instead, I planted the dekes in two grass clumps above the bench. I draped the ghillie over my head and shoulders and called to a trio of distant gobblers. To tickle their ears, I needed a call with a high, sharp, and dulcet tone. Two Eddie Horton box calls were made to order. One is an Arkansas Razorbox, and the other is one I call "The Heirloom." It is made of red, blue, and gray laminate with a mahogany lid. Horton doesn't make it anymore, but it is the sweetest sounding call I own. I scratched out a few yelps from both, followed by clucks and purrs.

The breeze floated down the hollow, so I knew the gobblers heard me. I put the calls down and waited.

At 6:50 a.m., a gobbler thundered at the edge of the woods behind the pine tree. It was so close that it rattled my bones and jellied my insides. He was coming up the same route that the rat-smelling gobbler followed the week before. I was certain it was the same tom. I twisted to the right in my seat and shouldered my shotgun, which held a full complement of three-inch shells stuffed with 1 ½ ounces of Remington No. 6 Hevi Shot. My nerves jangled as a red and white head bobbed toward the clearing on the other side of the blackberry bramble. It was a legal gobbler, and another gobbler trailed him. Five more steps and the lead bird—President Madison—would step into the clear.

The second gobbler, the president's Secret Service detail, clucked, and both birds turned toward the woods. I called them back with a silky purr. President Madison approached the clearing, but his wingman turned him again.

"Don't go over there, Mr. President. That area has not been secured," he seemed to say, but I spun President Madison around with a purr and cluck.

Again, President Madison was about to step clear when The Wingman circled around the back of my tree. He clucked nervously, with increasing tempo and volume. President Madison reversed, and I knew I wouldn't turn him again. The birds balked as I staggered to my feet. At fifteen yards, a snap shot over the top of the briars put President Madison on the ground. He only weighed 18.8 pounds, but his beard was 10 ½ inches long. His spurs were one-inch and $^{15}/_{16}$-inch long. Only when I hoisted the flapping President Madison into the air did The Wingman finally will himself to leave his fallen comrade.

I walked behind my hiding spot to where The Wingman sounded his alarm. I got on my hands and knees and peered through the tangled vines and tendrils. The rising sun behind the bramble splintered the light into a million glaring shards. The Wingman couldn't possibly have seen me. I concluded that the decoys must have unnerved him. Still, I wondered, what did he see behind the tree that triggered his alarm? I will never know.

Emotions overtook me as I kneeled and said a prayer of thanksgiving. I have hunted, hiked, camped, and played under waterfalls with my family at Madison County WMA since 1987. I have a soul connection with the place, and to kill a gobbler there in such a dramatic fashion overwhelmed me. I shared the moment by text with friends all over the United States, including my mentor Mike Stanley.

"You've come a long way since ol' Woody gave us the slip," Stanley said in a text message. "According to the Game and Fish online harvest stats, you're the only hunter to kill a turkey at Madison County WMA this weekend. Congratulations, my friend!"

Knowing that I might never draw another Madison County turkey hunting permit, I couldn't bring myself to leave. I lingered long and etched every sight, sound, and smell to my sensory hard drive. I also set my camera on a tripod and shot a bank of photographs for my computer hard drive.

Back at camp, I hung President Madison from a limb and broke camp slowly, enjoying every moment of the sun-splashed morning. If this were indeed my last hunt on this place, it was one for the ages. It was everything a turkey hunt should be, and that gobbler was the most meaningful I've hunted.

Nonsense! I've said the same about them all.

Chapter Seventeen

GLORIOUS FAILURE

In Arkansas, a hunter may kill no more than two mature gobblers in a season. I had yet to tag out in my home state, but on the last day of the 2017 season, I believed it was finally possible.

According to the Arkansas Game and Fish Commission, fewer than one hundred hunters kill two gobblers in a typical season, but only about eleven percent kill even one gobbler. I tagged out with two gobblers in Missouri in 2004, and I've taken two-bird county limits in Oklahoma thrice, but in fourteen years of hunting in Arkansas, I hadn't come close.

The Lumberjack brought me halfway in 2017. So sublime was that hunt that I returned to the same spot on the last day of the 2017 season in hopes of replicating it. The sight of The Lumberjack strutting down a silver shaft of morning sunlight in the apse of St. Tom's Cathedral was the most beautiful thing I have ever seen in a lifetime of hunting. I dearly wanted to see it again, but scenes like that happen only once. The next gobbler, if there was a next gobbler, would write its own screenplay.

Unlike The Lumberjack's hunt, there was no reluctance, confusion, or indecision on the final day. I woke alert and eager at 4:15 a.m. The moment I stepped out the front door, I knew it would be a gold-frame classic. It was cool, clear, and bright, and the air was dead calm. It was ideal gobbling weather.

I rose a little earlier than usual because of a disaster that occurred a couple of days previously. I entered a large tract of twenty-year-old pine trees where I have never known a turkey to roost. True to my luck, I walked under the only tree in that entire parcel to hold a roosting turkey. A shockwave shuddered through my bones when the bird thundered out of the tree and crashed through the web of limbs in the gathering light. In Arkansas, you seldom get second chances, so I wasn't surprised to encounter no other turkeys that day.

On Monday, I veered wide around that area to avoid an encore. I settled into a good spot and made soft tree calls as I waited for dawn. Unlike the previous day's hunt, I left my turkey hen decoys in the bag because they almost prevented me from killing The Lumberjack. Decoys are assets on some hunts, but lately I regarded them as liabilities. Naturally, I shunned them on a day when they would have been helpful.

Sitting in the same spot as where I killed The Lumberjack, I called with a Premium Game Calls diaphragm and a slate call of unknown manufacture. I bought it in 2005 at a turkey hunting expo, and I never go afield without it. A glass top covers a rough slate upon which rests a breast feather from a Rio Grande gobbler. The top is mostly decorative, but a portion of the glass is textured to form a striker surface. With the right striker—and I sampled many to find it—the glass produces a high, clear tone. In the bottom of the pot is a recess that exposes the smooth bottom of the slate disc. It produces a deeper, raspier tone than the textured glass, and it is perfect for clucking, cutting, and purring.

As during The Lumberjack's hunt, I used an Eddie Horton box call made of black walnut and bloodwood. I also used a Furr's custom box call constructed of walnut and maple that was made in Scranton, Arkansas. It is number eight of twelve made to honor the late Gary Watts, who in 2015 became only the sixth person to be inducted into the Arkansas Turkey Hunters Hall of Fame.

A gentle soul, Watts was a giant in wild turkey conservation circles. He first joined the National Wild Turkey Federation (NWTF) in 1978 when he bought a box call from a hardware store in his hometown of Paris, Arkansas. Inside the call was an invitation card to join the organization. Watts became a major force in organizing and mobilizing turkey hunters at a time when wild turkey restoration efforts were finally bearing fruit in Arkansas. He served two terms as president of the National Wild Turkey Federation's state chapter. The Turkey Federation also honored Watts in 2010 with its Roger Latham Award, which it bestows on its most outstanding volunteers. Additionally, Watts founded the NWTF's Mt. Magazine Chapter, which was later renamed to the Gary Watts-Mt. Magazine Chapter.

The twelve limited edition calls were specially made for an auction at the 2016 Arkansas National Wild Turkey Federation annual awards banquet in Little Rock. Each call was auctioned individually for $200-$225. Along with the call, each winner got a poker chip with the same number as the call to be entered into a super auction for a Weatherby Orion over/under 12-gauge shotgun. One chip was drawn from a bucket at the end of the auction, and the owner of that chip won the shotgun.

The auctioneer asked me to draw the winning chip from a bucket. It was number 8, held by Jim Wells of Hamburg, Arkansas. In the exuberance of his good fortune, Wells handed me the call and shouted, "You can have the call! I got the gun!"

Wells, a casual acquaintance that I encounter at random times and places all over Arkansas, is a bit of a stealth mentor. I first met him by way of a phone interview for a turkey hunting article I wrote in the early 2000s about turkey hunting on Casey Jones Wildlife Management Area in southeast Arkansas. We met in person for the first time at the Arkansas State Turkey Calling Contest and Expo in March 2012 at Stuttgart, Arkansas. I was watching Preston Pittman, a noted turkey caller, go through his routine when I struck up a whisper exchange with a knowledgeable guy standing beside me. It was Wells. He explained the various stages of a competitive calling routine and pointed out where the imaginary turkey was and what it was doing as Pittman deployed his sonic arsenal.

Many elite callers don't use artificial calls. They use their own voices. I dearly wish I had the ability, but I don't and never will. Another guy used a pot call, or slate, for his routine.

"I don't see many people using pots in this competition," I whispered.

"Pot calls have built-in limitations, especially during an actual hunt," Wells said. "For one thing, it requires you to move your hands. Any movement when a turkey is close is a liability. In a competition environment, it's really hard to keep a fluid rhythm with a pot because of the back-and-forth motion. It causes little interruptions, hiccups, that you don't get with mouth calling. Not only that, but your striker is always making little tapping sounds, and that's a big no-no."

We listened. They were subtle, but delicate taps were certainly audible despite the caller's excellent pitch and cadence.

"That counts against you in a competition," Wells said. "You have to be really, really good to win a competition with a slate. It happens, but not very often."

A couple of years later in Fordyce, Arkansas, home of legendary Alabama football coach Paul "Bear" Bryant, I found myself standing behind Wells in line at a convenience store sandwich counter. We ate lunch together and talked about turkey hunting for more than an hour. It seems like whenever I need a turkey tutorial, Wells serendipitously appears to provide it.

I last saw Gary Watts in January 2017 at a tiny little gun shop out in the boondocks near Paris, Arkansas. I was there to buy a long-desired deer hunting rifle, a Browning A-Bolt Stalker chambered in 25-06 Remington equipped with a Ballistic Optimizing Shooting System (BOSS). The BOSS has an adjustable weight on the barrel that tunes the barrel's oscillation harmonics with the particular bullet you're shooting. It also has a muzzle brake that reduces recoil. It is a rare configuration for that rifle, and I was willing to travel to get it. It is also one of my most accurate rifles, and I used it to kill a magnificent old buck in 2018 in Mississippi, at Cottonwood Farm, a legendary hunting property where Will Primos, one of the outdoors industry's greatest entrepreneurs, built a hunting video empire.

Watts sat in a chair by a sun-soaked window drinking a cup of coffee. I joined him, never dreaming it would be the last time I would see him. He died two months later. Come April, I wanted to honor Watts by summoning a gobbler with the call that bore his name.

My Gary Watts commemorative call is different from the others I own. The wood is soft, so its tone is subtler and perhaps even a bit more textured than those with harder, more thoroughly cured woods. It's not exactly raspy. I would describe it as hoarse, and you really have to put pressure on it to get volume. Despite its quirks, it is effective in Arkansas's woods.

A few days after I killed The Lumberjack, I called up a hen at about 6:25 a.m. It was still fairly dark in the woods, and I was surprised to see a turkey on the ground so early. She probably tended a nearby nest.

As did The Lumberjack, a turkey gobbled from the direction of a nearby logging deck. I heard nothing in that area for several days after my successful hunt, so it must have taken awhile for a new gobbler to occupy the territory. Looking into the misty swirling light atop the hill, I hoped to see another backlit gobbler strut down the open lane. This gobbler approached from a different direction and locked in about 200 yards to my right. He was coming fast, so I shifted positions to gain a better angle.

His gobbles trembled the forest. The Lumberjack was a boomer. This one was a screamer with a raspy, cutting tone. He sounded like Little Richard belting out the opening lines to "Long Tall Sally." I aimed at a spot about twenty-five yards away where I expected him to appear, but two hens picked Little Richard off before he was in range. I did not see any of them again, but Little Richard gobbled for the next hour.

Hens and gobblers eventually separate when hens return to their nests, so I expected to summon Little Richard back between 11 a.m. and 1 p.m. He did not resurface, but three more turkeys appeared at 10 a.m., about a hundred yards away. One was a good gobbler, and one was a hen. I didn't get a good look at the third bird. They paused to acknowledge my calls, but they had a destination in mind. It is very hard to change turkeys' itineraries when they are on autopilot, but I tried valiantly by making fighting purrs with a pair of small finger yelpers.

Immediately after those turkeys departed, I texted Mike Stanley to ask him if the fighting purr was appropriate for that situation. Stanley says that the fighting purr is probably his most effective call. Reluctant gobblers in north Arkansas can't resist it, Stanley said, and in the years I've known Stanley, it seems to have helped put at least one bird on the ground for him annually. One turkey gobbled loudly at the fighting purr, but he wouldn't turn. I correctly deduced that the hen kept him tethered.

"My fighting purr usually works best on a lone gobbler or multiple gobblers without hens," Stanley replied.

Thank goodness for text messaging, the equivalent of sideline-to-press-box communications among members of a football coaching staff.

I had not been around so many turkeys since my glory years in Missouri. All I want is a chance, and the abundance of turkeys made me confident. The stage was set for the season finale.

Little Richard was up early the next morning for the final act, but he sounded noncommittal. A lot of other things were going on at that moment, and they all converged at once to actualize a turkey hunter's sweetest dream, or his bitterest nightmare.

As I conversed with Little Richard, another turkey approached slowly from behind. It made tentative, inquisitive clucks with a deep, raspy tone like that of an old alpha hen. Although I was between the hen and Little Richard, I didn't like competing with a live rival.

With the season on the line, Stanley's fighting purr was my money play. I simulated a protracted argument. Little Richard gobbled angrily and changed course. He was on his way and itching for a fight. The hen behind me was also approaching cautiously. I could not abide being jilted again, so I mimicked the hen's every yelp, cutting her off with utmost disrespect. Furious, she clucked angrily in response and with escalating irritation.

The ideal scenario would be for the hen and gobbler to arrive at the same time. However, the hen was about thirty-five yards away when my brain finally processed the signals in my ears. The turkey behind me was not a hen. A gobbler was making those deep, raspy clucks and yelps.

In front to my right appeared not one, but two gobblers. A third gobbler trailed them but remained concealed in brush. The dominant tom—Little Richard—chased his subordinate in a frantic serpentine course, pecking him every time he caught him. Those two gobblers were well within killing range, but they were at an awkward angle that would have required me to pivot and betray my presence. I expected them to cross in front toward my decoy, but the rearguard gobbler ruined everything. His advance slowed as he neared the spot where he expected the ersatz hen to be, and his clucks grew more spaced.

He finally stopped five feet behind me. That's right, five. Five-zero. His clucks sounded like fingernails on a chalkboard. The timbre and pitch of his clucks changed, from aggressive inquisitiveness to suspicion. The entire hunt teetered on the precipice of disaster.

Keep moving! I exhorted silently.

The rearguard gobbler needed only to take six to eight more steps forward to blunder in front of me and bring this act to a splendid climax. Instead, he anchored. The other two gobblers stood erect, their eyes locked on the rearguard gobbler and thus locked on me. The absence of a hen finally tripped all of the rearguard gobbler's trouble triggers. He retreated quickly in alarm, emitting "putts" that cued the other gobblers to disperse and run. Before I could select and sight down a gobbler to shoot, I was all alone.

Brother Mike apologized profusely in a text message. A critical detail that he omitted from his advisories, he said, is that dominant toms often do not gobble at a fighting purr. They come in clucking, like the rearguard gobbler did.

I was now on the plush chair side of my own desk subjecting myself to a withering performance review. I should have repositioned when I first saw Little Richard. The problem is that if you can see a gobbler, he can see you better. I did not know how close the rearguard gobbler was at that point, and because I mistook him for a hen until it was too late, I froze when I should have adjusted. In retrospect, I should have spun around to face the rearguard gobbler as soon as I heard him, but again, that would have required correctly identifying him as a gobbler.

I might have excused that error had it not happened twice before. Once was in Missouri, and the other was in Oklahoma sitting beside Glenn Clark. Even if the rearguard gobbler had been a hen, the other two gobblers would have joined her and walked in front of my gun barrel. It was a valuable lesson in case I am ever in that situation again. I claimed to have learned the same lesson the other two times, also, but this time it hurt bad enough to finally imprint.

On the other hand, it was the first time I had a chance to work four gobblers at once anywhere. To have happened in Arkansas was not just phenomenal, it was miraculous. The Eastern gobbler is said to be the wariest of the North American turkey subspecies, and to call one almost into my vest pocket was an achievement even without shooting.

As failures go, this one was glorious.

CHAPTER EIGHTEEN

LET'S SLEEP ON IT

Never underestimate the power of a nap.

In the summer of 1993, I was the outdoors editor at the *Morning News*, a small daily newspaper in Springdale, Arkansas. After years of rebuffs, I finally got an invitation to cover the prestigious 1993 Bassmaster Classic bass fishing championship. Covering the Classic was by invitation only, and it was a status symbol for outdoor writers. Those that regularly attended were an elite clique that the organization feted and pampered. The rest of us were serfs. Trend-setting professional bass fishermen ignored our requests for interviews, and the fishing industry disregarded us. A small coterie of writers set the agenda for the bass fishing industry, and the rest of us commented or reported on the trends and issues that they defined. An invitation into the Bassmaster Classic press corps elevated a writer to opinion-shaper status and conveyed a higher degree of legitimacy.

The Bass Angler Sportsman Society (BASS) noticed me in 1992 when the organization scheduled its 25th Anniversary Tournament at Beaver Lake near Springdale, site of the watershed tournament that established the mega-billion-dollar bass fishing industry.

In early 1967, Ray Scott, an insurance agent from Montgomery, Alabama, was in a motel room in Jackson, Mississippi, sulking over a rained out fishing trip, when he said he had a vision involving one hundred fishermen paying one hundred dollars to compete in a bass fishing tournament on Beaver Lake. Jackpot fishing derbies had been around for decades, but they were infamous for cheating and graft. Furthermore, Scott had never been to Beaver Lake or Springdale. He knew them only from a magazine article.

Scott, an indefatigable salesman, immediately traveled to Springdale and pitched his idea for a national bass tournament to the Chamber of Commerce. Presenting himself as the president and chairman of the nonexistent All-American Fishing Tournaments, he asked the chamber to underwrite the venture. The chamber refused, but Scott persevered and actualized his vision in June 1967. The success of that event gave Scott the impetus to establish BASS, which he built into an entertainment and media powerhouse.

For the 25th Anniversary Tournament, the *Morning News* assigned me to produce a promotional tabloid. I believed that Scott's participation was vital, so I blithely called his office for an interview. That was when I discovered that Scott, believing that he and BASS had been defamed in coverage about a lawsuit, had shunned the media. Scott's secretary told me adamantly that Scott would not speak with me. Ever.

"I am not interested in anything controversial," I pleaded. "I just want a few minutes with him to share his recollections of that first tournament. It's a huge deal for us in Springdale, and it's very positive for BASS as well."

"I'm sorry, but Mr. Scott is not giving interviews at this time for any purpose," said the receptionist coolly.

I tried several other angles, but her tone grew icily impatient.

"Ma'am, will you please just give him my name and phone number?" I asked.

"I have already told you that Mr. Scott is not speaking with the media," she said.

I could practically feel her telephone receiver descending to its cradle.

"Yes, ma'am, I understand," I said. "All I ask is if you will just give him my name and phone number. I am not asking for a single thing more."

"I don't see the point in that. He's not going to call you," she said, her resolve cracking.

"I understand, ma'am," I said. "I'm just asking if you will give him my name and number. Not a thing more."

"I'll do it," the receptionist said with a loud sigh, "but I'm telling you, it's not going to do you any good."

"Ma'am, a big part of my job is reading other people. From one Southerner to another, I know that you are a lady who keeps her word. I am grateful, and I thank you for your time."

Weeks passed, and I resigned myself to completing the project without Scott's input. I wrote and photographed all of the tabloid's content, but I held a space open in case of a miracle. I was eating breakfast at home one morning about a week before deadline when my phone rang.

"Is this Bryan Hendricks?" asked a gruff, grits-and-gravy drawl.

"It is," I replied guardedly.

"This is Ray Scott from Montgomery, Alabama. I have a message that you want to talk to me about the 25th Anniversary Tournament."

That interview lasted over two hours. I filled an entire Big Chief tablet front and back, and the story was the tabloid's centerpiece. Scott summoned me when he arrived in Springdale for the tournament, and with his arm around my shoulder, he personally introduced me to all of the luminaries in the bass fishing world. He gave me a copy of his book, *Prospecting and Selling: From a Fishing Hole to a Pot of Gold*, which formed the foundation of my freelance writing and photography business. All told, those few days I spent with Scott advanced my career at least seven years.

I asked Scott, "Of all the journalists in America, of all the people you know and trust, why did you call me, a nobody in Little Town, Arkansas?"

"Because my secretary put in a good word for you," Scott said flatly.

In the run-up to the 1993 Classic, a publicist at a well-known western wear clothier asked if I would consider riding with one of its sponsored anglers, an unknown kid from the Northeast who had qualified for his first Classic.

"It would be a neat angle for you, a small-town reporter covering a small-town angler," the publicist said. It was a tactful way of saying that nobody important wanted to cover the obscure amateur, and I was probably the last name on his list. I accepted the invitation.

The angler was Bryan Kerchal, a fry cook from Newtown, Connecticut, who qualified for the Bassmaster Classic as an amateur. That feat required beating about 40,000 anglers nationally who competed in a grueling circuit for a single berth in the Classic. The Classic's amateur qualifier was unquestionably the nation's best amateur angler, but an amateur had never fared well in the Classic. The talent gap between the pro and amateur echelons was perceived as too vast.

Because my sports editor needed my services to complete an annual high school football tabloid, I had to skip the 1993 Classic, so I did not get to spend that time with Kerchal. He finished last.

Had the story ended there, I wouldn't have missed much, but it didn't. Its continuation was one of the great disappointments of my career.

Kerchal's defining moment came one year later when he defied astronomical odds to qualify for the Classic as an amateur for a second time. His practice period at North Carolina's High Rock Lake suggested that Kerchal was due another dismal performance in the 1994 Classic. Exhausted and frustrated with his inability to decipher a productive fishing pattern, Kerchal put down his rod and took a long nap on the deck of his bass boat. When he woke, he noticed a discarded fishing lure floating in the water. He scooped it up and put it on a hook. He caught a fish, and then another. A pattern emerged.

On July 30, 1994, Kerchal, 23, became the only amateur to win the Classic.

On Dec. 13, 1994, Kerchal died in a plane crash near Morrisville, North Carolina.

Mike Iaconelli, an emotional, frenetic, break-dancing dreamer from New Jersey, also ascended through the amateur ranks into the Bassmaster elite before turning pro. Like all Bassmaster amateurs, Iaconelli idolized Kerchal. While preparing for the 2003 Bassmaster Classic in New Orleans, Iaconelli experienced such insurmountable adversity that he wondered if he even deserved to be there. Like Kerchal a decade earlier, Iaconelli put down his rod and took a long nap during practice. He awoke rejuvenated and inspired to win the Classic with one of its most memorable performances. The difference between Iaconelli and Kerchal was that Iaconelli was already a pro when he won his Classic.

In an earlier chapter, we established through other examples how good things come from naps. It is not debatable.

My 2018 Arkansas spring turkey season opened in disappointing fashion. As usual, I barely slept, but I rose with a sore throat and chest congestion. It was cold outside, but I would not allow it to sideswipe a day I had anticipated for so long. Fueling my dreams were vivid memories of the 2017 turkey season finale that ended with a close call involving four gobblers. That season also began with me killing The Lumberjack, my most memorable gobbler.

A modest run of success made me hungry for more success, but don't mistake hunger for greed. I had come so far from just a few years earlier when enduring failures had fostered a defeatist attitude that nearly killed my joy for the sport. Taking a few tough Arkansas gobblers had made me confident, but history, gratitude, and the inherent uncertainties of pursuing an avian paragon of suspicion kept me humble. Merely for the honor of having known them, I treasure the gobblers that escaped almost as much as the ones I killed.

Merely getting to the woods was a challenge that morning. I nearly collided with a horse that dashed into a blind curve and lost its footing on the slick pavement mere feet from my front bumper. I regard such occurrences as dual-edged omens. Being on the right side of a close call might portend good luck, but I also take it as a warning to be vigilant on a day when margin of error might be very thin.

Wearing a vest full of callers, I made the long walk to my pew in St. Tom's Cathedral, which had become an astonishingly productive turkey hunting location. Sunrise arrived in a wash of crimson, and I marveled at the shattered rays swirling in the mist. Atop the ridge across the ravine, a line of pine trees cleaves light into a V. Picture a rock concert with searchlights and lasers cutting through the smoke at an indoor arena when smoking was still allowed in public venues, without the distinctive aroma of marijuana, of course.

The memory of The Lumberjack strutting down the light shaft like a preening rock star was still vivid. I longed for April 10, 2018, to follow the same script, but I knew that it couldn't. Sublime hunts are like torrid love affairs that pound their stakes in your heart. You remember every kiss, every touch, every seductive whisper, but you also know that they're stitched to one partner at one place in time. No matter how satisfying or how merciless, they are doomed to pass, but another will always follow. A hunter remembers them all with equal passion and longing.

The Lumberjack was the "One" in his season. This season it will be another, and, lord willing, there will be another after that. Embrace the affair in hand, and prepare for the emotional shower of its blooming.

There was no love in the air that morning. Turkeys were on hiatus from my area, so I amused myself with my supernatural ability to summon crows with turkey calls.

At 9 a.m. I drove to town, fueled my truck, and ate breakfast before returning to camp. I felt terrible and consumed half a bag of lozenges to soothe my burning throat. Back at my hunting camp, the day had turned windy and warm, and it made me drowsy. I parked my truck in the sunlight, closed the windows, covered myself with a parka, reclined the seat, and dozed. For me, this is a proven cold and flu therapy. I wrap in layers and sweat out the affliction. The evidence is anecdotal and scientifically dubious, but I swear it works.

I was despondent when I woke at 1:40 p.m. I had missed the critical 11 a.m. to 1 p.m. window when gobblers and hens separate. Having bred their morning's escorts, gobblers go on the prowl for new mates. I was so discouraged that I considered going home.

It's too late and too windy, and I feel awful, I thought. *Maybe tomorrow will be better.*

Of course, tomorrow would not be better, nor would the day after. My schedule was packed, and I couldn't return until Thursday.

In a journalist's world, any number of things might pop up before then to disrupt my plans. I remembered opening day of the 2013 season on this property when I called up two big gobblers and killed one at 4:13 p.m. There was plenty of time for good fortune left in this day.

I'm here, I thought. *May as well try to make a play.*

I returned to my pew in St. Tom's Cathedral and discovered that the deep woods were relatively calm. It should be the kind of place turkeys would seek in windy conditions. I laid out my usual array of callers, which included two Eddie Horton box calls, two slate calls made by Grant Westmoreland and David Taylor, both of nearby Sheridan, and a Premium Game Calls diaphragm made in Dierks. Arkansas gobblers deserve Arkansas-made calls, but I also had a Pope's Pock'et Call from Alabama.

I played them to no effect, and then played them again fifteen minutes later. A gobbler replied close behind me. The risk of repositioning was too great, so I sat still and hoped the bird would walk in front of me. Those were the opening moves of a chess match that lasted slightly longer than an hour.

The tom went long silent after that first gobble. The quiet initially unnerved me, but I relaxed and cleared my head. The turkey was probably standing behind me looking for a hen. He would stare until I moved, and that would spoil the hunt. I'd ridden that horse in my early rodeos, and I did not intend to get bucked off again.

My experiences in such situations usually involved a bird moving in quietly and announcing its presence by spitting and drumming. If that were the case, I would hear it step through the crunchy forest litter. After about fifteen minutes of blood-surging silence, I concluded that the turkey had departed. I said a little prayer requesting success and then repeated my litany of calls in an attempt to sound like a flock of hens.

The tom gobbled, but it had crossed the ravine in front of me to an opposite ridge about 200 yards to the southeast. I continued calling, and the gobbler answered aggressively. Finally, I saw him. He was in full strut descending the side of the ridge, brilliantly illuminated in the afternoon sunlight. It was a different quality of light than at the morning service, but the gobbler itself was as resplendent as The Lumberjack. The waving grass shimmered, creating a near dreamlike effect that made the gobbler appear like a mirage.

Inexplicably, the gobbler pulled in his feathers midway down the ridge. He stood erect, scanned my ridge and abruptly reversed course. He continued gobbling, but he was singing a Dear John dirge. It was time for the secret weapon. I pulled two finger yelpers from a pocket and made a fighting purr. The gobbler howled and reversed course again.

Despite my pleadings, the gobbler refused to leave the opposite ridge. He pranced back and forth bellowing at my every call, but the ravine seemed to have the effect of an electric fence. A decoy might have persuaded him, but I stopped using decoys the year before after they nearly cost me a shot at The Lumberjack. Unable to see hens, this gobbler's interest ebbed, and he drifted away again to the southeast.

It was time for my double-secret weapon. I used a deep-toned Horton box call to produce an artificial gobble by quickly scraping the lid both directions across the case. Eddie Horton showed me how to do it, but I'd never gobbled before because I feared calling up another hunter. I had done all I could do conventionally. Gobbling was my last option.

The faux gobble grievously offended the tom, but he still refused to leave his ridge. I cut off a gobble with a mouth cackle. I did it again, and again, and again, and again. A quintuple gobble! Three were the most gobbles I had ever provoked from a tom. He was hot, and the impertinent hen and an unseen rival were too much for him to abide.

The gobbler descended the ridge and headed straight my way. A second gobbler emerged from the brush and joined him. The urgency of the previous moments melted away. The second gobbler's arrival seemed to calm the first bird, and they acted as if the hen were an afterthought. They pecked at little morsels as they zigzagged down the hill, interrupting their noshing to scan my hillside. I was anxious to speed them up, but a little voice stilled me.

"The Good Lord's got this, Bud. Stay out of the way," it said.

Eventually the turkeys disappeared in the ravine. I shouldered my Winchester SX3, but they didn't reappear.

The Lumberjack had done the same thing and nearly escaped. I fought panic. These gobblers could exit the ravine either direction, and I would never see them again. The same little voice that stilled me earlier said, "Do it. Now!"

I pursed out a soft yelp with my diaphragm. The dominant gobbler replied, but he was still below the rim. His bass tones raised every hair on my body. Seconds later, a gobbler cleared the rim. At 3:18 p.m., my Winchester brought down the curtain on this superb act.

The second turkey sprinted back up the hill, wings outstretched and putting. As I suspected, the bigger gobbler was the escapee. I killed the subordinate gobbler, but I was in no position to be choosy. It was him or nothing. I chose wisely because they were the only two gobblers I saw or heard all season. My bird sported an 8½-inch beard . . . and ¾-inch and ⅞-inch spurs. I didn't weigh him, but he felt like 50 pounds after the one-mile walk back to the truck.

Only then did I remember my sore throat. It was gone.

CHAPTER NINETEEN

TAGGED OUT AT HOME

Next to the fighting purr, the American crow might be my favorite turkey hunting accessory.

I'm not talking about a crow call that hunters use to provoke toms to gobble on the roost. I'm talking about a live crow, like the one that saved my hunt on opening day of the 2019 Arkansas spring turkey season.

Crows are annoying. We enjoy the melodic songs of the cardinal, wood thrush, and sometimes even the insults of the blue jay. The crow is like the greaser teenager blasting AC/DC through his speakers on an otherwise peaceful day at the park. At best, they're casual nuisances. Heaven help your ears if a crow discovers a hawk or an owl nearby. A flash mob will form, screeching and shrieking and swarming until it overwhelms and vanquishes the intruder. Crows live to raise hell, and they love nothing more than a riot.

A gathering of owls is called a parliament in deference to their mythical wisdom. A group of crows is called a murder. It is an appropriate descriptor. Crows devastate pecan crops, and they prey on the nests of other birds that we like. I once watched a crow perch in a lone tree in a cutover near a wild turkey's nest. When the hen ventured out to forage, the crow swooped down and raided the nest. It made me angry.

Once, while crappie fishing at Lake Hinkle near Waldron, Arkansas, I watched a hawk abscond with a baby crow that it snatched from a nest. The crow pursued the hawk with wails of unmistakable anguish, trying valiantly to force the hawk to drop the chick. I admit to having felt sympathy for the crow, but karma's a bitch.

Crows and wild turkeys have a tense relationship. In 1997, I accompanied Arkansas Game and Fish Commission (AGFC) wildlife biologists on a turkey trapping expedition in the Muddy Creek Wildlife Management Area in the Ouachita National Forest. The mission was to trap a flock of turkeys, record the birds' vital data, and then release them. Preparations were laborious, beginning with a long, spine-compressing ride to the test site on the back of an all-terrain vehicle with Laurel Moore, an AGFC biologist. A technician certified in the use of explosives arranged a battery of small rockets attached to a net around a site baited with corn. When the turkeys concentrated in the middle of the bait site, the technician would fire the rockets to cover the bait site with the net to capture the entire flock.

We waited for hours in blinds for turkeys to arrive. Since my role was to photograph the event, I had a blind to myself to accommodate my equipment. Hot, bored, and tired from waking at 3:30 a.m., I napped for most of the day. I woke several times to hear my companions laughing at my snoring.

Late in the afternoon, a few turkeys appeared near the bait site. A few more joined them, followed by a few more. Rocket Man was moments from firing the net when a group of crows strafed the turkeys, grabbing at them with their feet and screeching while hovering over their heads. It wasn't malicious, really. The crows wanted the corn. They dispersed the turkeys and chased them back into the woods. Our mission was aborted and an entire day wasted because of a dastardly murder of crows.

My attitude toward crows began to soften while hunting with a friend in northern Arkansas. During a midday break, we visited a family that had rehabilitated and domesticated an injured crow named Ivan. He was the charming but clamorous czar of the deck, holding court from his throne atop the back of a patio chair and demanding tidbits from a boy enjoying a grilled cheeseburger.

About that time, I read *Indian Captive* by Lois Lenski. It is the story of Mary Jemison, who was abducted in the 1700s by a Seneca raiding party. A Seneca woman praised the crow that, despite its mischief and impudence, protected the village by warning of danger.

Influenced by that story, I began paying closer attention to crow vocalizations in the woods, mainly because crows often announce the presence of other animals in their territories.

Many times, crow shouts have roused me from inattention during uneventful deer hunts. Deer appeared soon after, and thanks to the crows, I was ready for them. I learned to distinguish crow social vocalizations from alarm calls and intruder calls. When crows shout at a deer, for example, it's more of an acknowledgement. With bobcats and coyotes, they sound indignant. With raptors like hawks and owls, it's a call to arms. When crows shout at turkeys, their tone is taunting and disrespectful. I learned to view crows not as adversaries or allies, but as double agents. After all, they'll rat on me with equal vigor if they discover me. I consider them a live alarm system, or maybe a stern schoolteacher who forces me to be extra still and quiet. Those are good attributes for a turkey hunter.

Therefore, I am happy to join crows in the bleachers for opening day of spring turkey season, which is like opening day of baseball season for sports fans. Every hunter is undefeated, but the last thing you want is a rain delay or, worse, a rainout. On Sunday morning I was disappointed and anxious to see that the weather forecast called for rain until about 10 a.m. By Sunday night, the chances of rain diminished. By Monday morning—April 8, 2019—the threat of rain all but evaporated.

A choir of chuck-wills-widows greeted the dawn, yodeling over a string section of songbirds. Cardinals joined in as the woods brightened, and I surveyed the pine-studded diamond to visualize how the toss of the ceremonial first pitch would unfold. Would it be a crowd-pleasing strike, or would the pitch sail over the catcher's head to the backstop, eliciting laughter and jeers from the bleachers? I paid my usual respects to the memory of The Lumberjack, the Hall-of-Fame gobbler that walked the aisle through the light of St. Tom's Cathedral, and then I got down to business.

Like the year before, I did not bring a turkey decoy because I believed that decoys had been liabilities in previous early-season hunts. When a male turkey sees a decoy, he often veers away and expects the "hen" to follow. If he doesn't see a hen, he keeps searching, and he usually comes much closer. Eliminating the visual lure removed what I had come to regard as a complicating variable. Eliminating decoys as a crutch also forced me to rely more on my calling. Technically, I don't consider myself to be a particularly talented caller, but I have refined my ability to "talk turkey." As my friend Jim Wells once said, "Some of the awfullest sounding calls I've ever heard came from real turkeys." You just have to be convincing enough to override all of a gobbler's defenses.

As the dawn brightened, one gobbler sounded between a recently thinned pine thicket and me. Another bellowed to the north, followed by another to the southwest, and yet another. Being roughly between two or more gobblers is advantageous because gobblers will often race to a yelping hen. Instead, these gobblers all went away, probably because they already accompanied hens.

As usual, I had a selection of calls, including the Arkansas Razorbox made by my friend and mentor Eddie Horton. I call that box "Corliss" in honor of Corliss Williamson, an all-American forward on the Arkansas Razorbacks 1994 NCAA championship basketball team. His nickname was "Big Nasty" because of his aggressive play in the lane and his instinctive ability to score against and defensively neutralize bigger opponents. The Arkansas Razorbox, with its nasty, raspy tone, is the "power forward" on my turkey calling roster. I also had an Eddie Horton box call with a bois d'arc base and a cherry lid, as well as a selection of Premium Game Calls diaphragms, a Premium Game Calls Diamond Cutter slate, and a David Taylor slate.

As usual, I played all of the callers to mimic a flock of hens. Around 8 a.m., an irate hen arrived on the opposite ridge. She cutt and cackled angrily. I answered her note for note hoping a gobbler would follow, but the hen was alone. She descended into the ravine in front of me, ascended my side of the hill, and passed five yards to my right. With my face concealed behind a mask and my eyes concealed behind bronze Oakley sunglasses, I was invisible. She cutt and yelped all the way across the flat until she vanished into a thicket about 300 yards behind me. The same thing happened about forty minutes later. Those two hens taught me a lot about vocal sequencing, and I practiced their routines all day.

At about 10 a.m., the woods settled into their midday lull. A raccoon crossed the fire lane and crows poked around in the pine duff. Mike Stanley, who was hunting up north in Sharp County, exchanged text messages with me all morning about our observations. He said gobblers were probably loafing or dusting in the shade. Turkeys in repose are unlikely to come to a call, so I took a break and went to town for lunch.

I returned to my spot at 2:20 p.m., far later than I liked. As I walked, I recalled my last Oklahoma hunt when I bumped into a group of gobblers dusting near my blind at about noon.

As I neared my set, I saw three jakes on the opposite ridge at the same time they saw me. In a bout of adolescent indecision, they scampered in circles and figure-8s before galloping over the ridge. I continued walking and saw a mature gobbler about eighty yards from where the jakes had been. He sped away, and I excoriated myself for returning so late to this place. You don't get away with that in Arkansas. If you bust one bird, you've probably ruined that spot for the day. If you bust four birds, you've probably ruined that spot for a week and maybe for the season. With only a sixteen-day season, the margin of error is exceedingly slim.

I considered relocating, but with gobblers moving, I didn't want to compound my errors. Besides, I had killed two gobblers on this property after 3 p.m., so I said a little prayer and asked the Good Lord to absolve my turkey hunting transgressions and to bless me with an opportunity to work a gobbler. I never pray to kill a bird. I only pray for an opportunity. I waited about thirty minutes to reset the board, and then I struck up my one-man band.

Before 4 p.m., a gobbler bellowed to the north and left a sound trail that followed a wide arc to the east and then to the south-east. The tom entered my orbit, but he was resolutely going away. Eventually, the gobbler went silent. I assumed it went into a nearby cutover and that the hunt was finished. Nevertheless, I didn't want to risk bumping the bird on the way out and spoil my chances of working him in the morning. As I calculated an exit strategy, a crow plummeted through the pines and screeched about seventy-five yards away. A shock gobble thundered in response. Apparently, the tom was drifting my direction in a lazy arc. Besides gobbling at the crow, he refused to maintain a dialogue, so I was never certain of where he was.

To help loosen his tongue, I deployed my secret weapon, Stanley's fighting purr. The tom gobbled wildly throughout the sequence, but he sounded again as if he had veered away. It was time to pass the ball inside to Corliss and see if Big Nasty could muscle that bird out of the paint. Corliss made a few cutts, cackles, and yelps, and those did the trick.

The gobbler turned. He was coming. I heard him drum and drag his wings, but he was invisible over a rise. I couldn't discern his path nor predict where he would appear.

His easiest approach was on the grassy firebreak in front of me, but turkeys don't always follow the easiest route. My options were limited, and the tom was probably too close for me to shift positions. After a short wait, I yelped softly on the diaphragm. The tom gobbled from the fire lane, probably no more than forty yards away. He had the ball and was dribbling toward the goal. I shouldered my gun and waited for him to drive to the hoop.

After what seemed like a pressure-packed eternity, I saw the gobbler's bright red head bee-boppin' behind a brushy curtain. When I saw the beard, I knew he was legal. At 5:08 p.m., my Winchester SX3 ended the game with a rim-rattling slam dunk. Of course, I credit Corliss with the assist in the box score.

Kneeling over the bird, I said a prayer of gratitude. Bronze-tipped feathers glowed in the sunlight as a soft breeze rustled through the pines. I didn't weigh the gobbler, but his beard was exactly eleven inches long.

My iPhone chimed with an incoming text message from my friend Mike Romine, who was hunting about a half a mile away.

"Was that you a few minutes ago?" Romine asked.

I texted him a photo of the bird.

"You a turkey killin' fool! Congratulations!" Romine replied.

After checking the gobbler on the Game and Fish Commission's mobile app, I followed the gobbler's incoming path out of the woods and bumped a hen into flight at the far end of the fire lane. To my knowledge, that's the only time I've ever called a gobbler away from a hen. That made the hunt especially sweet, but I wouldn't have had a chance without help from my good buddy the crow.

Three days later, I returned to the same place, but conditions were diametrically different. Distant thunder rumbled, and misty drizzle presaged an approaching thunderstorm. Violent gusts roared through the pines, filling the air with pollen so dense that it looked like yellow smoke. The chance of a gobbler hearing a call in such a fierce wind was beyond remote. The chance of me hearing a gobbler was even more remote. Nevertheless, this was the only time I had to hunt for the rest of the week, and frankly, there was no other place I would rather have been, bad weather or not.

Having failed to wake in time for a morning hunt, I arrived at 12:30 p.m. So meager was my confidence that I brought my laptop so I could write my Sunday newspaper feature. It started out as a mood piece about the sights, sounds, and musings of an uneventful afternoon in the turkey woods. Writers keep this theme in reserve because as much as we hate to acknowledge the mercenary nature of our profession, any outing that doesn't produce copy is time wasted.

I also packed two Rhodes box calls, including a two-chamber walnut model that Bill Rhodes made specially for me in 2012. The other is like it but made of cedar and with the chamber lengths reversed. Loud, raspy, and resonant, they excel in windy conditions.

During writing breaks, I checked an Arkansas social media hunting site on my phone where hunters pleaded for advice on how to hunt turkeys in the wind. The posts came from every corner of the state. The consensus opinion was that turkeys go into fields in the wind and that they are highly unlikely to be in the woods except in protected ravines. My hunting spot overlooked a protected ravine. It continued into a dense thicket that extended nearly half a mile. If it wasn't the right spot, it was at least the right kind of spot.

Between gusts, I yelped, cutt, and cackled with the box calls. One thing I love about the Rhodes calls is that I can make a sharp cutt and then drag the lid over the opposite lip to make the quavering yelp that I once heard two hens make. Still, I needed something extra. I texted Stanley and asked, "Ever used a fighting purr as a locator to shock a gobbler?"

"Absolutely, and sometimes it's all that will work," Stanley replied. "Like rattling for whitetails, you need to be ready to set up quickly. Gobblers tend to be like bucks when responding to a simulated fight. They either come racing in looking to rumble or sneak in quietly to look over the competition."

I tried the fighting purr and continued playing the Rhodes boxes. At about 1:40 p.m., I thought I heard a faint gobble pierce the gale. I quickly hit the box, and another faint gobble responded as the gust subsided. The gobbler continued to respond to my calls. He didn't sound any closer, but I recognized his voice. It was Little Richard, the screaming gobbler that I worked in 2017 before finally killing The Lumberjack. Little Richard was at least two years old in 2017, so he would have been at least four years old in 2019. That would make him the undisputed king of these woods.

Anticipating the customary marathon that defines many of my turkey hunts, I continued tapping on my laptop in a state of relaxed readiness. At the next break in the gusts, I did an extended fighting purr. Little Richard bellowed twice during that exchange, and I resumed typing.

He gobbled again, and he was much louder.

Oh, hell, he's coming! I thought.

Softly, I shut the lid on my laptop and slipped it under my arched legs. I lowered my mask and raised my shotgun. Little Richard strolled blithely in front of my sights, and at 2:10 p.m., I put him down at fifteen paces. It was the shortest, easiest, and most uneventful hunt of my life.

Little Richard was a grizzled old warrior. He weighed twenty-one pounds. His beard was exactly 9 ½ inches long, but his spurs were 1 ⅛ inches long and as sharp as needles. His wingtips were worn square from strutting. His plumage, especially his breast feathers, was sparse and disheveled from breeding and fighting. In comparison, the gobbler I killed on opening day had an 11-inch beard, but his spurs were short and blunt. So immaculate was his plumage that he looked like he'd just left the tailor.

On one level, I felt rueful for Little Richard to have fallen so easily, especially after having to work so hard for his less experienced counterpart. On the other hand, an easy hunt made me appreciate the hard ones even more. With great relief and satisfaction, Little Richard also required me to rewrite my feature. The revised edition was much more compelling.

In a notoriously hard state to hunt wild turkeys, I had just killed my seventh mature gobbler in seven seasons, four while sitting in the pew. I tagged out for the first time, the ultimate goal for any turkey hunter and a rare accomplishment for an Arkansas turkey hunter. I felt ecstatic to finally crest that mountain yet humble, knowing that I might never do it again.

As the thunder grew louder, I tucked Little Richard into my vest and surveyed my pew in St. Tom's Cathedral, unaware that the spirit had departed. Little Richard was the last gobbler to sing in its choir.

CHAPTER TWENTY

THE HOLDOUT

I n the turkey hunting zodiac, western Oklahoma is a Gemini. It's hot and cold, yin and yang, sweet and sour, maybe or maybe not.

In addition to wild turkeys, Roger Mills County was once one of the nation's premier quail hunting destinations, the training ground where Steve DeMaso and Danny Pierce taught me how to hunt quail in 1999. Long periods of prolonged drought in western Oklahoma devastated not just quail but also deer, turkeys, and fisheries. Large reservoirs dried to dirt, and the hardest hit areas lost an entire year of white-tailed deer reproduction. Young turkeys, desperate for water, drowned in stock tanks by the scores.

When rain returned in 2015–16, quail recovered to their heyday, and the number of year-old turkeys was prodigious. That set the stage for a parade of turkeys that tested my resolve and rewarded my patience. Ironically, it also marked the end of western Oklahoma's glory era for turkey hunting.

Late in the 2016 spring turkey season, Glenn Clark and I made our biennial turkey safari to a windswept expanse of rolling sandhills near Sweetwater on the Texas border. Joining us was Justin Ammons of Dallas, Texas, one of Clark's colleagues at a marketing firm that represents major outdoor gear manufacturers. Ammons, an avid bowhunter, brought only a small longbow made by Dan Toelke, a custom bowyer in Montana. It is an elite bow for an elite archer.

"I showed up to a goose hunt with my bow, and the guide got mad about it," Ammons said. "By the time I shot half a limit, he was on the phone gushing about it to all his buddies."

Ammons had a reputation in the bowhunting world before he went to work in the hunting industry, but a crass challenge from a television producer changed his career arc.

"He said, 'Let's see what ya got, Mr. Best-Instinctive-Shooter-on-the-Planet,'" Ammons said, recalling the incident. "He threw up a clay target, and I hit it twice. I put my bow down and walked away."

The producer chased Ammons down and said, "If you can shoot a bow like that, I'd love to see what you can do with a camera."

Ammons was a disillusioned, burnt-out church youth minister low on emotional fuel and yearning for an exit. That video gig gave him a front-row seat on some epic hunting adventures. As a product rep, he gets the best of all worlds.

As usual, we stayed in Willard Gilley's cabin near Sweetwater. Touring hunting properties with Gilley, we saw turkeys in almost every field. A few strutters escorted hens, but there were also big flocks of jakes and hens.

One spot—a hillside in a field of bluestem tallgrass near a cow pasture—looked especially attractive. A wooded fence line was about a hundred yards away. Another wide stretch of prairie was on the other side. Of course, a field you see for the first time in daylight looks a lot different in the dark. I couldn't find my spot the next morning, so I sat in a small grove uphill from a creek close to the road from which I had entered.

At dawn, gobblers chuckled from every direction. A hen pitched out of a tree right over my head. Shortly after, I called up a gobbler of undetermined age that veered away and vanished into the creek bottom.

At about 8 a.m., a turkey on the other side of the small rise answered my yelps. I clucked softly and purred, but a lack of response started me daydreaming. About twenty minutes later, I felt a presence. I looked up at a flock of eight jakes and ten hens staring down at me from the crest of the hill just fifteen yards away. I sat statue still hoping a mature gobbler might join them. None did, and finally the flock strolled down the opposite side of the hill and reappeared in the clearing by the creek. I belly crawled to the top of the hill and identified all of the jakes through my binoculars. I picked out the tallest birds with the longest beards, for lack of a better term. They were more like nubs. I kept my sights on them for twenty minutes, aiming at one and another, trying to will myself to pull the trigger. With so many turkeys about on the first day of a hunt so late in the season, I was bound to see a mature gobbler eventually, and probably more than one. I lowered my gun and watched the turkeys through my binoculars until they meandered out of sight.

It is hard to let a gobbler walk away because I always fear it will be the last gobbler I see. On the other hand, if you settle for young gobblers, young gobblers are all you will get. Advanced deer hunters adhere to the same ethic in regard to killing young bucks rather than waiting and working for mature bucks. As a turkey hunter, I have conditioned myself to let the young ones walk, but temptation is relentless.

I finally found my spot after lunch. It was a brush blind about a half a mile from the road in a natural convergence point for three types of cover. To my great delight, bobwhite quail were omnipresent. They surrounded my blind, and a pair almost came inside. Also, a prairie kingsnake entered my blind and slithered over my boots before exiting on the other side.

An hour later, a hen walked out of the woods and got within six feet before she finally saw me and fled. A gobbler sounded off in the distance, and I responded with a fighting purr. Instead of summoning the gobbler, I started a boisterous argument with a boss hen in a nearby thicket. She cackled angrily, and I enraged her by repeatedly cutting her off. I expected her to charge into the clearing to thrash the invisible upstart, and she would certainly bring a big gobbler with her. She stopped at the edge of the field, and she did not emerge.

At about 4:20 p.m., I heard yelps up the hill. I responded with clucks and purrs on an Eddie Horton box call made of bois d'arc with an ebony lid. The instrument is an artistic masterpiece, and its deep, raspy tone projects well in open country. Two jakes strolled into the clearing. It was almost closing time, and my standards had relaxed. I put my bead on one jake and then the other, trying to determine which was bigger.

The internal conflict raged anew. Did I really want to kill a jake so soon? Did I want to kill a jake at all? It was only the first day, after all. I have two more days. A mature gobbler is bound to show up eventually.

On the other hand, he might not. I might not see any more jakes either. I came a long way and sat out here a long time to leave empty handed.

"Stick with your game plan," I told myself. "This country is crawling with turkeys!"

With my luck, I'd kill a jake and then spend the next two days covered up with mature gobblers. It's turkey hunting's variation of "Let's Make a Deal." A guaranteed shot at killing a jake in the field is Door 1. I could let him walk and wait for a mature gobbler. That's Door 2, an all-expenses-paid vacation. Or, I could return to my morning spot tomorrow and try to call up two mature gobblers. That's Door 3, an all-expenses paid vacation AND a new car!

Having failed to call a vocal gobbler to that spot this morning, I had no reason to expect a different result in the same spot later. Therefore, Door 3 afforded the lowest odds of success. The odds for Door 2 were not demonstrably better. The odds for Door 1 were imperfect only because of the possibility of missing the shot, but given my desire to bag only mature gobblers, it was also an unsatisfactory option.

On the other hand, the old saw about the bird in the hand didn't emerge from the ether. I guarantee that a turkey hunter coined it in a situation identical to this one.

As that debate raged in my head, the jakes stood erect, cocked their heads, and eyed the tall grass. They parted aside as a massive gobbler sauntered into the clearing. At twenty yards, my Remington V3 put the big Rio Grande longbeard on the ground with a blend of Nos. 5-6-7 Hevi Shot. Its beard was 10 ¼ inches long. Its spurs were 1 inch and 1 ⅛ inches. The time was 4:37 p.m.

That was the only gobbler for our group. Ammons called up a gobbler that did not come close enough for an archery shot, and I declined to shoot a jake from a flock of five the following day. It was also the first time I didn't tag out while hunting with Clark in Oklahoma, but it wasn't the last. Clark and I returned in 2019 to a different world, and we wondered if it would ever be again as we remembered it.

My 2019 visit with Clark was our fifth Oklahoma hunt together since 2010, and I was ecstatic after a superlative season in Arkansas. Our enthusiasm waned when our outfitter warned us that hunting had been very tough because of precipitously low turkey numbers. I have hunted this area since 1999 when Roger Mills County was at its turkey hunting peak. I have photos from 1999 showing fields loaded with 125 to 150 turkeys. The country teemed with turkeys, but media people like me put the word out, and hunters came from all over the country to get a piece.

A familiar and predictable pattern ensues every time a new turkey hunting hot spot emerges. Wildlife management agencies set game limits and season lengths to ensure sustainable game populations while also providing maximum hunting opportunity. Limits are based on a complex formula that factors the habitat's ability to support the animals coupled with the amount of hunting pressure game animals can withstand from the number of licensed hunters in an area or region.

Nonresident hunting pressure is additive and is generally inconsequential except when it comes to wild turkeys. Turkey hunters are the most avid subset of the hunting community, and regardless of their economic status, they travel.

The gold rush starts when hunting magazines publish breathless accounts of working veritable flocks of uneducated gobblers. You read some of it earlier in this very chapter.

It goes something like this: "I had my pick of half a dozen 10-inch beards! If I blew one opportunity, I knew I wouldn't have to wait long for another! At sunrise, the tremulous symphony of no fewer than twenty gobblers roosting along the cottonwood bottom tickled my ears!"

The articles climax with the hunter choosing the biggest gobbler from a flock of giants, all but promising the same to any who follow.

Bag limits are traditionally generous, especially in Plains states that regard turkeys as lightly as they do prairie dogs. Until recently, for example, Rio Grande turkeys were so plentiful in western Oklahoma that the Oklahoma Department of Wildlife Conservation did not require hunters to report turkeys they killed west of I-35. Game checks are the only tool wildlife management agencies have to estimate the number of animals that hunters kill, but western Oklahoma was so rife with turkeys that the state wildlife agency apparently thought the bonanza was eternally limitless.

Celebrity hunters sponsored by sporting goods manufacturers come from all over the country to make videos that help sell their sponsors' products. Of course, they always hunt with and promote commercial hunting outfitters who lease large amounts of property and book as many hunters as the calendar allows. Outfitters believe that they have not only leased the hunting rights to the property but also the rights to the game therein. If one hundred gobblers inhabit a property, the most rapacious outfitters infer the right to kill them all.

Landowners are indifferent. They raise cattle, hay, and other crops. They often regard wild turkeys as nuisances at worst and peripheral assets at best. To them, hunt lease money is simply additional income from an incidental resource that helps pay their property taxes.

Meanwhile, wild turkeys are inextricably vulnerable to natural variables such as drought; flooding; poor hatching and brood rearing conditions; and predation from coyotes, bobcats, raccoons, skunks, owls, hawks, crows, snakes, and everything else that eats turkeys and turkey eggs.

When overhunting depletes a local turkey population, an outfitter abandons unproductive properties and moves on to exploit the next good place. In time, cumulative pressures overwhelm the resource, and turkey populations crash. Turkey hunters continue coming for a few years before the truth becomes undeniable, and then they descend on the next hot spot. Sometimes turkey populations recover. Sometimes they don't. Arkansas, for example, has experienced this ebb and flow cycle twice since the late 1980s.

Harvesting wild meat for commercial consumption has long been illegal, but commercial recreational hunting is an extension of the profiteering that devastated North American wildlife populations in the late 19th and early 20th centuries. Whenever a market monetizes wildlife, wildlife suffers always and without exception. Until state wildlife agencies regulate the nonresident hunting of turkeys with the same respect as they do big game animals such as deer, bighorn sheep, elk, mountain goats, and bears, then turkey populations will fluctuate at the mercy of the commercial hunting market.

All of this, including my contribution to it as a hunting journalist, dogged my thoughts as I contemplated the relative dearth of turkeys compared to our previous hunts. One tends to take his opportunities for granted in the good times, but diminished opportunities are especially glaring when you've traveled far to a place in decline.

Still, memories of the good times buoyed our optimism on the Monday of my last Oklahoma spring hunt with Clark in 2019. The temperature was about fifty degrees at dawn. It was very windy with a threat of rain. As we descended into a creek bottom, Clark asked if I had an owl call. He'd scarcely uttered the words when a real owl hooted in a tree above us. Silence ensued.

"That's not a good sign," I said. "If a real owl doesn't provoke a gobble, there's probably not a gobbler around. At least not right now, there isn't."

Clark set up on a big sandy dusting area that contained a lot of scratch marks and even a few turkey droppings.

"Something will show up here eventually," he said. "This is probably my best shot."

Crossing the creek, I eased through a rough area of tall grass, cedar trees, and sagebrush. It was the prettiest turkey habitat on the property. Creeping a step every ten seconds, I froze when a dove burst out of the grass about fifteen yards ahead of me amid a frantic thump of wingbeats. Inches behind its tail feathers was the outstretched paw of a bobcat, claws extended. I waited, stone still. About three minutes later, the grass parted about six feet in front of me. The bobcat registered surprise, then puzzlement, and then alarm in the two seconds it took to process the sudden appearance of this camouflaged interloper. The cat vanished in a blink.

In the evening at another property, a big gobbler eluded Clark by walking on the wrong side of a shinnery mott as it exited a field.

"He'll go back to that field tomorrow evening," I said. "If you get in front of the shinnery, it won't matter which way he goes. He'll have to pass you first."

We had one more day to hunt. Relaxing at the lodge watching Roxy Music, The Cure, and The Zombies perform at the Rock & Roll Hall of Fame induction ceremony on television, we sipped legally distilled moonshine from plastic cups.

Clark said, "Every time we do this, I get so pumped when I book the hunt. Then, as it gets closer, I think, 'Why am I doing this? I don't have time! I'm too busy!' And then we get out here, and I'm like, 'I am having so much fun! Why don't we do this more often?'"

I laughed and said, "It's the same way with me! You know how it is. We keep on "Shinin' On," brother!"

Touching cups, we toasted our last attempt to bag what seemed to be the last gobbler in Roger Mills County.

I was not familiar with the farm's configuration, but I knew Clark hunted near a natural gas well that he said was on the opposite side of the farm diagonally from where I hunted. The wind and rain ebbed about 3 p.m., and calling conditions were much better. All was quiet on my end of the farm, so I prepared to search for a turkey.

I texted Clark. "Are you up near some loud machinery running?"

"I can hear something, but it's a ways off," Clark replied.

The din came from a natural gas well about a half-mile up the hill from my spot. If Clark couldn't hear it, then that meant he was on the far side of the farm. I had this whole side of the farm to myself. I forgot that Clark has significant hearing loss from too many nights in blues clubs and from playing amplified music at home and in his church. Throbbing machinery would not register with him nor would he hear a turkey gobbling in a nearby field.

But I heard it. It sounded like peals from a distant church bell.

As I crept through the shinnery, sage, and cedar between my original location and the gas well, faint gobbles grew increasingly clearer. About a hundred yards in front of me was a ridge with some bushes on top. The gobbler raised hell on the other side. A field had to be over that ridge.

I belly crawled through stickers and sand burrs for a peek over the crest. Indeed, a massive gobbler strutted and bellowed at the far side of a big field. Then I glanced to my left. Up the hill, beside the gas well, was a bright reflection. Through binoculars I saw that the glare came from the windshield of Clark's truck. I had tracked down Clark's gobbler, which meant that Clark had to be somewhere near. I wouldn't budge until I ascertained his location.

"Is a gobbler near you?" I texted.

"No," Clark replied. "I haven't heard him in a while."

"What do you mean you haven't heard him?" I texted. "He's gobbling like a son of a bitch right down the hill from your truck!"

I was puzzled. Clark had to be closer to him than I was.

"I see your truck. Where are you?" I texted.

"About two-hundred yards down the hill from the truck," Clark replied.

"Straight down in front of it?" I texted.

"Yes. I'm in the second thicket."

"Is that your bird strutting in the field?" I texted.

"I can't see the field," Clark replied. "Must be. If you see him, do your magic!"

I cutt and cackled. I interrupted the turkey's gobbles. I even gobbled with a box call. My fighting purr usually closes the deal with reluctant gobblers. I did it twice, but the gobbler strutted in circles while hens darted all around him. Finally, the gobbler folded his feathers and followed his hens out of the field.

"He would have come to a fan decoy," I said afterward. "I can't believe I left it at home."

"There were really fresh tracks in the sand," Clark said. "His spurs left little pin pricks in the sand, kind of like a buck's dew claws. I think I got there about thirty minutes too late."

"We've got him pinpointed," I said. "If we had one more day, we'd get him."

"It would mean getting home really late, but we could do it," Clark said.

"You know what? As tempting as that is, knowing we've got him is good enough for me," I said. "As scarce as turkeys are in this country right now, it would give me no joy whatsoever to kill that bird. He's doing exactly what he needs to be doing: making lots of little baby turkeys. Let's come back when they've got some gobblers to spare."

CHAPTER TWENTY-ONE

CROSS TIMBERS

S pring 2020 arrived at the onset of a global coronavirus pandemic that cryogenized the world.

The mysterious disease that in February was rumored to have killed untold numbers of people in Wuhan, China, seemed a remote threat until about 9 p.m. on March 11. I was enjoying a Karbach draft lager in a Little Rock restaurant with my broadcast partner Ray Tucker after the conclusion of our weekly radio program. Our Wednesday night routine included a raucous sports conversation with a loquacious bartender over a pizza and beer. Pepperoni, mushroom, and beef topped my half of the pizza. Tucker's side contained pepperoni and Italian sausage, along with a side of Captain's Wafer crackers and the restaurant's signature dressing.

Above the bar, a television showed the University of Arkansas Razorbacks defeating Vanderbilt in the first round of the Southeastern Conference (SEC) college basketball tournament. The crowd in the arena was sparse, which is common for an early conference tournament game. Already, the virus was firmly entrenched in the nation's consciousness, and the broadcast team discussed the possibility of restricting fans from the remainder of the SEC Tournament and even the National Collegiate Athletic Association (NCAA) Championship Tournament.

On March 12, 2020, the dominoes began to fall. The SEC and other major athletic conferences canceled their tournaments. The NCAA also canceled its men's and women's basketball tournaments. The NCAA men's tournament is a premier sporting event and a major economic driver. The NCAA suspended and then canceled its baseball season. The National Basketball Association canceled the remainder of its season. The Professional Golf Association canceled its tour. The bad news came in waves.

Overnight, the sports department at the *Arkansas Democrat-Gazette* had nothing to cover. On March 12, I was on Lake Ouachita interviewing Stephen Dunlap, an Iraq War veteran who was participating in a kayak bass fishing league tournament. My phone jingled an incoming text message. It was from my boss, Jason Yates. He wrote that for the foreseeable future, the sports section would be "All Outdoors, every page, every day, so get BUSY!" Thank goodness he ended the text with "LOL." Yates had actually planned to fish with me that day, but the cascade of sporting event cancellations had chained him to his desk.

To his credit, Arkansas Governor Asa Hutchinson endorsed fishing and other forms of outdoor recreation to promote emotional and physical health within the structure of coronavirus social distancing protocols. Yates's text message underscored the sobering fact that Outdoors was the only live beat remaining in the sports world.

By default, mine was also the de facto voice for the state's hunting and fishing community, which was increasingly anxious about the potential restriction of hunting and fishing activities at the dawn of their peak season. They had good reason to be concerned. To prevent people from congregating, the U.S. Army Corps of Engineers closed campgrounds, day-use areas, and swim beaches on Corps reservoirs. Fortunately, the Corps kept boat ramps open, allowing its waters to serve as pressure relief valves for all of the people who were suddenly out of work with plenty of free time on their hands.

On April 2, 2020, the National Parks Service closed the entire Buffalo National River to prevent large congregations of primarily Arkansas nonresidents. In the process, the Parks Service also restricted fishing and turkey hunting along the 135-mile long river and its corridor, one of the state's most popular destinations.

Anxiety mounted for turkey hunters who had booked trips to Kansas, Nebraska, and Texas. On April 5, the Nebraska Game and Parks Department announced that it had suspended the sale of nonresident turkey hunting permits to discourage nonresidents from entering the state. On April 10, the Kansas Department of Wildlife and Parks followed suit. Turkey hunters worried that the U.S. Forest Service would follow the Corps of Engineers' example and restrict hunting on national forests. Ultimately, the national forests remained open, but Arkansas hunters worried that the Arkansas Game and Fish Commission would close the spring turkey season for nonresidents and residents alike.

"The Game and Fish Commission cannot close turkey season," I wrote in a column. "That would be utterly demoralizing."

The 2020 Arkansas turkey season remained open, but it was utterly demoralizing on its own merits, producing yet another in a long succession of dismal harvests compared to those in neighboring states. One neighbor, Oklahoma, was particularly kind to me over the years, and there I opened my 2020 season with the hunt of a lifetime at a place called Cross Timbers Wildlife Management Area (WMA).

Owned by the Oklahoma Department of Wildlife Conservation (ODWC), Cross Timbers WMA covers about 10,000 acres of post oak-hickory woodlands in Love County near the Texas border, not far from Lake Texoma. Gently rolling ridges define the topography. Despite frequent use of controlled burning, its woods are dense. A few small creeks flow through the area, and there are many ponds. The ODWC maintains vast amounts of cultivated food strips within the WMA for wildlife, and it also leases grazing rights to local cattle ranchers. Cattle disturb the soil and mimic the effect that buffalo once had when they roamed free in that country.

The Oklahoma Wildlife Department regulates turkey hunting at Cross Timbers WMA through a random drawing similar to that used for controlled-access turkey hunts on Arkansas WMAs. It awards only ten permits annually, which translates to one hunter per 1,000 acres. Fewer than half kill a turkey, which minimizes pressure on the birds and helps keep numbers prosperous. As a neighboring landowner said during a roadside visit, "If they ever open it up to where everybody can come, it'll be ruined in one year."

Having applied many years for a Cross Timbers turkey permit, I was ecstatic when I received notice that I had finally been selected. In fact, I checked the permit several times in the ensuing months to make sure I hadn't misread yet another rejection. Claiming the permit was a tricky process, and I almost forfeited my spot by over-looking the final step in the claim procedure. A final glance at the congratulatory email revealed my error, which I corrected a week before deadline.

Like Arkansas, Oklahoma did not quarantine during the pandemic as rigorously as other states. Brandon Carter, manager of Cross Timbers WMA, said that the Oklahoma Wildlife Department had no plans to shut down nonresident turkey hunting, but he urged me to arrive as soon as possible in case the situation changed.

"If we do close it, we will allow you to hunt if you're already here," Carter said.

The hunt dates were April 8–12, 2020. I arrived early on April 5 and claimed the best site in the WMA's designated campground, which was empty. The days were already very hot and humid, so I erected a canvas canopy over my teardrop camper to thwart the sun and provide a dry place to enter and exit the camper in case of rain. I brought a Yeti cooler full of food and drinks. I had ten gallons of fresh water, a half-gallon of milk, coffee, hot apple cider mix, and a bottle of fine bourbon. I hung two Coleman lanterns from stands, unpacked a camp chair, and settled in for a relaxed, comfortable vacation.

The days were anything but relaxed. This was a once-in-a-lifetime opportunity, and I did not intend to fail. On April 6, I woke at 5 a.m., filled my Thermos with coffee and walked a long trail to the WMA boundary. I tramped along the fence line to a high spot where I stopped, sipped my coffee, and listened. Nearby on the WMA boundary was a small house from which a distant flock of guinea fowl protested my presence. About an hour after dawn, a gobbler sounded off and took up a station on a ridge a half a mile away. I created a waypoint on my GPS and entered that bird as a strong possibility for opening morning.

After breakfast, I visited a different part of the WMA in a light rain. Zack Smith, an ODWC wildlife technician, pulled up beside me in his truck as I walked on the WMA's main road. I unfolded my map of the area, and Smith gave me a quick but thorough overview about what I could expect to see in various sections. He recommended a clover field near the area headquarters, but he warned that it had been hunted hard during a two-day youth season that ended Sunday.

"Turkeys like it in there, and there's a few that roost nearby," Smith said. "I see a lot of hens. I don't see many gobblers, but you know how that goes. If you see hens, you're bound to see a gobbler eventually."

Smith also pointed to a corner on a different part of the map. He marked an X with his pen.

"There's an old gobbler that roosts on private property right here," Smith said. "That's a bird you can probably call onto the area."

I visited the vicinity of the clover field at about lunchtime. Two toms in a wooded ravine seemed to be having a gobbling debate. I tailed them from a distance, but instead of entering the clover field, the gobblers went up a hill on the other side of the ravine and topped the opposite ridge. I visited Smith, who was preparing a tractor for his afternoon chores. I described the gobblers' behavior, particularly how they stayed in thick woods instead of entering the clover field.

"I bet I can get one of those gobblers, but I think you're right. They don't go in the clover field," I said. "My best bet is to intercept them in that little hollow that drains into that bottom. I have a feeling they follow the same route every day."

"You're probably right," Smith said. "I'll tell Brandon so that he won't send any other hunters down there. Good luck!"

In the afternoon, I scouted a section on the north side of the WMA. Nothing I saw there looked attractive, and I deleted that area from my list of possibilities. It was a good decision because that was where almost all of the other hunters concentrated on opening morning.

For my last day of scouting, I rose before dawn and stood by a pond about 200 yards from the clover field. No birds gobbled, and none entered the field, which I scanned with binoculars. Without turkeys to occupy me, I noted the things I saw on the pond bank, including a lid from a can of smokeless tobacco and a length of fishing line containing a bobber and bream hook looped over a low limb above a log in the water. I wrote a column for the newspaper, weaving a story around these disparate items as John Steinbeck did with refuse he found in a motel room wastebasket in *Travels With Charley: In Search of America.*

From the brightness of the cork and the fade of the tobacco lid, I assume that the same person did not deposit these items. The snuff user probably scooped the last dip from his can and dropped the lid. Doubtless, the container is nearby, probably buried in the mud.

That back right pocket of that angler's jeans bears the telltale ring of that peculiar addiction, and he or she probably wore scuffed and faded brown, square-toed Ariat boots. Somebody that discards smokeless tobacco spoor on a pond bank doesn't deserve to catch any fish.

The bobber in the tree is the reminder of a parent and child snatching a few elusive minutes from a hectic schedule. The parent works too hard and too long. The child has always got something going on, baseball, soccer, and other activities, which scarcely leave time to breathe. Coronavirus and its social distancing mandates put the brakes on their treadmills and forced them to slow down and hopefully appreciate some of the finer things in life, like sneaking away to a fishing pond.

The limb overhangs a fallen treetop that stretches far into the water. Bream and bass love places like that, but the dang limb makes it darn near impossible to land a cricket in just the right spot. You know how it is with bream rigs. The bobber makes the length of line topheavy, and the split shot unbalances the rig at the other end. It tries to go end over end when you flip it, and inevitably the hook and sinker loop over one of the higher limbs. The bobber snags in a small fork, stranding the rig. There's no way to reach it by hand, so the only thing to do is break it off.

Here's hoping they brought extra hooks, sinkers and bobbers so they could retie and continue. Perhaps they found a better spot and caught a big mess of palm-size bluegills. It would be a shame if they had to end the trip on account of the accident because quality fishing time is so hard to find. Coronavirus and its social distancing mandates will end soon, and people will go back to their old routines.

Having that much time to pen such an expansive idyll meant that the clover field was probably a poor choice for a morning hunt. It was clearly a midday option that I intended not to need.

On a hunch, I scouted the vast middle portion of the WMA in the vicinity of a 160-acre private inholding. The landowner runs cattle on the inholding, and its composition is slightly different than that of the public land surrounding it. That constitutes a disturbance as well as edge habitat, both of which attract game.

Abutting the south boundary of the inholding is an impenetrable wetland that would be a safe place for turkeys to roost. From here, turkeys leaving the roost could go straight to the inholding or pitch off the other direction to a ridge.

Bordering the west side of the inholding is a long food strip that ascends two hillsides, including one that abuts the west side of the inholding.

I was prepared to walk all the way to the south boundary of the WMA, but that proved unnecessary. At about 9:30 a.m., a gobbler bellowed atop the hill before me. He gobbled continuously, leaving a sonic bread crumb trail as he traveled through the woods on the ridge. Beyond the crest, out of sight, he crossed the strip and continued gobbling on the other side.

He probably travels a little circuit through here every day, and there's not a soul back here to bother him, I thought.

Of the many miles I walked, I knew I had finally found my magic spot. I've had that feeling in only two other turkey hunts. Once was in western Oklahoma hunting with Glenn Clark, when I foretold Clark that I would kill a gobbler while sitting against a blue barrel. The other time was in 2016, when I bagged President Madison. No doubt, Cross Timbers WMA was alive with turkeys, but they were elusive. I finally found a spot that radiated positivity.

I returned to camp and took a long nap. When I awoke, it was nearly one hundred degrees. I stuffed two decoys in a backpack and carried them and my ground chair up to the place near where I thought the gobbler crossed the strip. I left the pack leaning against a tree. That token of commitment would prevent me from changing my mind, and it would also relieve me from carrying a heavy load to the woods in the morning. I took a GPS reading so I could find it in the dark.

On the way back to the truck, I clocked the route. At a fast clip carrying no weight, it took forty-five minutes. I imprinted every rut, every dip, and every turn in the trail to memory so that I could confidently retrace my steps in the dark. That was unnecessary because the predawn moonlight was exceptionally bright.

On Wednesday, the first day of the hunt, I rose at 4:30 a.m., filled my Thermos with coffee, and made the short drive to my entry spot. I didn't need the GPS. I walked straight to my pack and placed the decoys in a woodland opening near the strip, oriented so that the morning sun would shine directly on their sides.

I am always so nervous and indecisive when I hunt in the mornings. No matter where I sit, that place over there is better. But what if a bird comes in from that direction? I need to be over there instead. Well, hell! I can't see well enough from there, and there's not a big enough tree to make a comfortable backrest. That's a better spot over there! Before long, I've bounced around to half a dozen setups.

Finally, I forced myself to relax, found a big tree that gave me a good view, and prepared to work a gobbler.

That's about the time a pack of coyotes yipped their version of reveille. Two coyotes can sound like twenty, but this bunch really did sound like twenty, and they sounded too close for my liking. I didn't fear them. I just didn't want them to mess up my hunt.

I hadn't used decoys for several years, but I believed they would be valuable here. Over time, I have observed that a lone gobbler often stops and displays about fifty or sixty yards from decoys. He expects hens to follow him, and he often refuses to come closer. In this situation, I only knew a gobbler was in the area. I hoped that decoys would provide a visual element to draw him close.

At about 7:45 a.m., I heard a faint gobble to the south. It sounded like the same tom I heard the day before. I moved fifty yards to the south, sat against a big tree, and extracted from my vest two Eddie Horton box calls, including one I call the Heirloom. It has a high, clear, sweet tone. The other is made of black walnut from Ouachita County, Arkansas, with a bloodwood lid from Africa. It has a high, raspy tone. I picked them from a dozen I brought to camp because they sound best in these woods.

I learned a new call before leaving for that hunt. It's a feed call consisting of a three-note whine followed by a short purr. I make that with a mouth diaphragm, but I had to try about a dozen models to get one with the right pitch.

I worked the two boxes and made a few cutts with the mouth call. The gobbler replied. A minute later, he gobbled again. He was committed, and he was closing fast.

Right about then, I heard and then saw movement to the right. Eight large feral hogs had appeared about twenty yards away. I waved at them. Instead of fleeing, they stared. This was a very bad development that reminded me of a muzzleloader deer hunt at Moro Big Pine Natural Area WMA in south Arkansas. I had sat at the edge of a natural gas pipeline right-of-way when I heard footsteps crunching in the woods behind me. I raised my gun and prepared for deer to appear. Instead, a small herd of feral hogs trotted out and stopped about twenty-five yards to my left. The largest, a boar weighing nearly 300 pounds stared at me and clicked its tusks aggressively. Sitting on the ground with no protective cover or even any trees big enough to climb, I was vulnerable. A muzzleloader gave me one shot. If that didn't disperse the swine, I could be in serious trouble. I shot and killed the tusk-clicking boar. The other hogs fled. I gave the pig to a group of hunters that happened along. The leader of that bunch said he would take it to a processor and have it converted to pork. We exchanged business cards, and he promised he would send me a portion of bacon and chops. I never heard from him again.

For this Oklahoma rematch, my shotgun held three shells, but shooting at these hogs would ruin the turkey hunt. I waved harder at the swine, but they continued to stare. They finally ran when I lunged at them and threw a stick. First coyotes and now wild hogs. If I hadn't spooked this gobbler, it would be a miracle.

About one minute later, the tom gobbled again. He was close enough for me to deploy the feeding whine. He responded with a double gobble. He came in running, but when he saw the

225

decoys, he buried his heels in the dirt and skidded to a halt. He displayed, snood dangling well beneath his beak. When he turned to face me, the sunlight illuminated his fan, making the buff and metallic green highlights glow like a velvet Elvis.

Even though the gobbler was fifty yards from the decoys, he was only twenty yards from me. I blew a light cluck with my mouth call. The gobbler pulled in his feathers, stood erect, and faced me. At 8:05 a.m., my Winchester filed the first report of the Cross Timbers WMA controlled turkey hunt. The Rio Grande longbeard was my first triple-bearded gobbler. The beards were 9 ¾, 6 ¼, and 5 ½ inches long, registering 21 ½ inches of total beard. The spurs were ⅞ inches.

After checking my bird on the ODWC's mobile app, I stuffed the gobbler in my backpack and hoisted it onto my shoulders. I put the decoys in my hunting vest, slung it over one arm, and carried the shotgun with the other arm. I cut some distance by taking a short-cut through thick brush and high grass, but it was definitely more arduous in heat that was already above eighty degrees.

Despite the heat and the weight, it was a very pleasant walk. I took my time and savored every step, knowing I would probably never see this place again.

Chapter Twenty-Two

CORONA CARL

As a lifelong Beatles fan who never fully relinquished dreams of being a touring musician, I sometimes indulge teenage fantasies about rocking a virtuoso performance in front of an approving Paul McCartney. The turkey hunting equivalent happened at the end of the 2020 Arkansas spring season.

My timeless hunt at Cross Timbers WMA set the stage for what I was certain would be an epic season in Arkansas. From 2013–19, I killed at least one Arkansas gobbler in every season except 2015, including seven in the same general area on the Old Belfast Hunting Club in northern Grant County. Four I killed sitting in the exact same spot, including a pair of gobblers I killed in 2019 to fill my first season limit.

A year had changed a lot of things in my enchanted forest. Loggers clearcut about 120 acres on the other side of a nearby road, removing about half of the mature timber in that area. A hill in the middle of that timber was a favorite roosting spot for turkeys, but logging reduced it to a moonscape. Obviously, the new configuration changed the way turkeys use the area. An identical situation occurred in 2015 on 120 acres to the south of my woods, and turkeys didn't come back until 2017.

For the first fourteen days of the sixteen-day 2020 season, I did not hear a gobble. I did not hear nor see a hen nor even a feather. My only evidence of a turkey was a set of half-day-old tracks in wet dirt.

I request only a chance. A gobble gives me a chance, however remote. A hen gives me hope for a chance. After about a week of sitting in silent woods, I went mobile. I hunted new areas on the property that were equally devoid of turkeys and turkey sign.

By the second week, my enthusiasm waned. I began leaving the woods increasingly early. I abandoned morning hunting. When midday hunting proved fruitless, I hunted only in the late afternoons. As the dull days dragged on, my interest ebbed and my dedication faltered.

A downside to writing about hunting and fishing for a living is that I need action and drama to produce compelling copy. Poetic musings about songbirds, sunrises, and reflective introspections are like seasonings with no meat. They quickly get as tedious to read as they are to write. My beat is rich in April. White bass are running. Trophy brown trout are biting. Streams are in peak floating and wading condition, and smallmouth bass fishing is peerless. Bream and crappie are biting. Largemouth bass are in every stage of their spawn from north to south, west to east, providing enough grist to fill my section twice a week. Two weeks of sitting alone in woods uninhabited by turkeys makes me painfully aware that I could and probably should be doing a lot of other things that would be more productive. I feel like I'm wasting time, and wasting time depresses me.

Simmering in this stew of professional inadequacy, I was resigned to being shut out at home when Brother Mike Stanley called.

Stanley, my coach and mentor, has a lot of friends in Arkansas, including one that offers respite from the emotional rigors of pastoring by offering Stanley solace in his Marion County cabin. Stanley's friend describes himself as having once been "not worth killing." Whatever the vice, he embraced it. Drugs, alcohol, womanizing, and brawling were the pillars of his lifestyle. He was a classic north Arkansas rogue. Under self-described conviction of the Holy Spirit, he abandoned his former life and devoted his future to Jesus Christ. Reborn, he made millions in his contracting business, but he said his wealth is a gift from God that he is obliged to share.

Generously, he offers his lodge to Stanley for a few days every spring so Stanley can recharge from the spiritual, physical, and emotional demands of his ministry.

It's not your stereotypical Ozark cabin of warped planks and cedar shingles, but instead a massive steel structure with a wood exterior that can resist a tornado. In addition, Stanley's friend owns a parcel of prime turkey habitat that he allows only Stanley and his son to hunt. Stanley had also experienced miserable luck in his home woods of Sharp County, so the landowner graciously offered a chance for both of us to end the season on a high note at his place.

On April 26, 2020, Stanley and I rendezvoused at Yellville. Although we communicate frequently via text messages, email, and phone, it was the first time we had actually seen each other in about two years. In the embrace of plush chairs at the lodge, we colored in the gaps. Stanley and I first hunted together in 2008, during a light-ning-streaked deluge in which we hadn't the faintest hope of encoun-tering a turkey. From that moment he became a close friend, advisor, counselor, and strong shoulder to prop me up in times of profound grief and loss. He is always the first to contact me on the anniversary of my son's death, but always several days before, just to let me know that his thoughts and prayers are with my family before the waves break over the desolate beach of longing and melancholy. For this spirit, he is widely known and highly regarded.

While his profession doesn't afford much time for outside activities, Stanley devotes what little he gets to hunting. His speciality is hunting mature white-tailed bucks with archery equipment, but hunting turkeys is his deepest and most enduring passion. We are roughly the same age, but my first turkey hunt was in 1999. Stanley was a turkey hunting pioneer in Oklahoma in the 1980s. He killed his first turkey in 1984 in Sequoyah County, and he killed his second gobbler in 1985 in Cherokee County.

Accompanying Stanley on that hunt was a neighbor who was locally prominent. When they returned home to Adair County, a game warden drove past as Stanley hoisted the gobbler from the back of his borrowed pickup truck. Turkey season was closed in Adair County, and the stern warden demanded an explanation.

"I was young, just a kid, really," Stanley recalled. "He scared me so bad that I would have confessed to anything. Fortunately, my neighbor vouched for me and convinced the warden that I killed the bird legally in an open county."

In 1986, Oklahoma opened turkey season in Adair County, and Stanley killed that county's first legally taken turkey in modern times. He wrote an article about the feat for *Turkey & Turkey Hunting* magazine.

"I was as green as a gourd, but I was the only person around that had killed a turkey, so everybody looked at me as an expert," Stanley said, chuckling. "One by one, the men in my church asked me to take them hunting and teach them what I knew, which wasn't very much. It really was a case of the blind leading the blind, but by some miracle I managed to call up a few birds, and they managed to kill them. And they were able to branch out on their own. We became known as the Turkey Hunting Church."

For his generational influence, one could rightly aver that Stanley is one of the fathers of turkey hunting in eastern Oklahoma.

Micaiah Stanley is Mike's son and soul mate. Micaiah, who pastors a church in Seymour, Iowa, exhibits the same traits that enable him to serve long in the same pulpit. He is also a seasoned hunter who may be even more accomplished than his father. Turkey hunting is also his passion, and he specializes in hunting on public ground, the sport's most difficult arena.

During our only hunt together as a trio in 2008, the Stanleys and I hunted a clever old bird named Woody that was far too wily for me. My errors ensured that none of us killed him. During a conference after Woody escaped, Micaiah said, "I'm going to leave y'all to it and see if I can find some better turkeys to hunt."

As I relived the story, Mike laughed and said, "Micaiah said, 'I could have killed Woody. I had him in my sights, but I wanted Bryan to get him.'"

"All that accomplished was to make sure that Woody died of old age, with lots of little baby Woodys running around," I said.

"Well, you know . . ." Stanley said, diplomatically tailing off without further comment.

The Stanleys could easily have dismissed me as a dilettante. Instead, they coached and encouraged me. Mike and I have spent hours talking about turkey hunting, emailing about turkey hunting, and exchanging text messages about turkey hunting, often while hunting. Whenever I get a gobbler, he is the first to know about it.

During his early hunts in Oklahoma, Stanley refined his preferred technique of hunting on the move. He slips through the woods stealthily, calling sparingly, listening, and then advancing on a talkative turkey. One of his techniques is the Yo-yo. When a tom gobbles, it's often an invitation for an unseen hen to join. However, a gobbler often gets anxious when a hen moves away, especially late in the season when hens are tending nests. If a gobbler will not come, Stanley moves closer and calls, and then retreats about a hundred yards and calls again. Then, he advances toward the gobbler about fifty to seventy-five yards.

"He will come toward a hen that's moving away, but he will still keep his distance, expecting her to come to him," Stanley said. "I'll run up closer to where I think he'll hang up, and I'll be right in his wheelhouse."

Traditionally, turkey hunters sit against a big tree when a gobbler approaches. Because of a deteriorating back ailment, Stanley seldom sits.

"Most of the turkeys I kill anymore I kill standing up against a tree," Stanley said. "As thick as the woods are that I like to hunt, when you see him and he can see you, he's only going to be twenty yards away or so."

My tactics are diametrically opposite. If I am confident turkeys are in an area, I will sit in one spot all day. Bob and Jodie Gilmer of Forum, Arkansas, imprinted that ethic in me on Oct. 31, 1987. My wife, Laura, and I were early into a yearlong backpacking adventure from Arkansas to Maine, and we had stayed the previous two nights at Withrow Springs State Park near Huntsville, Arkansas. An article about us appeared in the *Madison County Record*. While we hiked north on Highway 23 toward Berryville, the Gilmers passed us in their pickup truck. They jerked their heads around, braked hard on the road shoulder, and asked if we were the couple they'd read about in the newspaper. They invited us to spend the night at their home, and turkey hunting dominated the night's conversation.

The Gilmers were fanatical turkey hunters, and Jodie was adamant in her belief that it is unethical to chase turkeys.

"A real turkey hunter sits and calls a gobbler to him," she said. "Only slobs run around and ambush turkeys!"

Since the Gilmers were the only turkey hunters I knew at that time, I adopted their dogma as gospel. I became somewhat apostate over the years because circumstances sometimes demand that I reposition on a bird that insists on going someplace else. I am not above trying to outflank a gobbler if a situation requires it, but generally I find a spot I like and put down roots. If I can provoke a tom to gobble, I am confident that I can call him in close, even if it takes hours.

In my mind, the sit-and-wait method requires sounding like a flock of hens, and that requires using a lot of different callers. My vest typically carries at least two box calls. I carry as many as four friction calls. One has an aluminum surface, and one has a copper surface. Another has a solid slate surface. The other has a glass surface on one side and a slate on the bottom. I also carry four diaphragm calls and two wooden finger yelpers that you operate by pushing blocks that slide against a friction surface. These make Stanley's signature fighting purr. I also carry a novelty device called Pope's Original Pock'et Call. It looks like a hollow snuff can with chalked edges that make turkey tones when scraped with a small block of cedar.

My routine is to play all of the devices every fifteen or twenty minutes. If a gobbler is within earshot, he will hear the tumult. Eventually, he will come in for a look.

"I wish I could hunt like that, but my back won't let me," Stanley said. "I have to be up and moving, or my back will lock up on me."

"If a gobbler's not around, it's a lonely way to spend a day," I said. "It's an all-or-nothing proposition, but it's also a numbers game. If you stay at it long enough, odds are somebody will come calling."

On Monday April 27, Stanley and I entered a field ringed by at least eight gobblers. They were the first gobbles I'd heard in Arkansas since 2019. Stanley showed me a big cedar tree with an open spot next to the trunk under a protective canopy of branches.

"The way you like to hunt, I almost guarantee a bird will pass by here sometime today," Stanley said. "I'll be on the hill behind you to see if I can get one to play."

Stanley put out my hen decoy and placed a strutting gobbler decoy beside it.

"It's the first time I've used a decoy this year," Stanley said. "I have a love-hate relationship with these things, but a lot of times it seals the deal on these late-season gobblers."

After Stanley melted into the woods, the pace of the gobbling quickened as the toms prepared to leave their roosts. The gobbler's timbre across the field changed, indicating that it was on the ground. Two on the ridge flew past and landed in the bottom of the field, but I couldn't see them because the slope was too steep. I clucked and purred quietly with an Eddie Horton box call to let them know a hen on the hillside wanted some attention.

Unfortunately, I worked up a sweat hurrying to this spot on such a muggy morning. My face mask funneled my breath onto my glasses and blinded me. I removed my glasses, reasoning that any turkey that topped the hill would be close enough for me to see its beard unaided and determine if it was an adult gobbler. Minutes later, three red and white heads poked over the ridge at a range of about thirty yards, but their chests were not visible. Worse, my astigmatism made them look like apparitions in a Claude Monet painting.

The toms did not like that gobbler decoy. They stared at it for about five seconds before one tom peeled away and dropped out of sight. The others quickly followed, leaving me sorely disappointed and muttering. One of my cardinal rules is to never leave yourself to anyone's mercy. That includes allowing no one, no matter how dear a friend, to dictate how and where you hunt. As the emotions of the moment faded, I acknowledged that Mike had put me in a good spot and that only an eyewear malfunction prevented the hunt from ending quickly. Nevertheless, I got the distinct feeling that this spot had produced its lone opportunity for the day. Another minute there was a wasted minute.

For the next hour I gazed at a giant cedar spoil pile in the southeast corner of the field. It called my name loudly and beckoned me with a come-hither woody finger. With the field empty, I stashed the gobbler decoy in some brush, gathered my gear, and hastened down the hill. As a bonus, I found an opening in the pile behind a low shield of horizontal cedar limbs that was just big enough for my ground chair. The spoil rose about eight feet behind, ensuring absolute invisibility. I placed my hen decoy about twenty yards away and waited.

At 9 a.m., what appeared to be a big hawk sailed straight to me from about a quarter of a mile away. It was nearly on top of me when it dropped its tail and landed gracefully beside my decoy. It wasn't a hawk, but a hen turkey.

Well, Honey, you sure are a lot prettier than that plastic doll, I thought. *Take off your coat, and stay awhile!*

The hen fed for about fifteen minutes and departed.

At about 10 a.m., two jakes entered the field from my left. They ignored the decoy and never paused, but it was encouraging to see turkeys on the move. An adult gobbler was bound to show up eventually. I texted these happenings to Stanley, who reported zero contacts in the woods.

At about 11:30 a.m., a gobbler answered my calls from across a creek. For almost two hours he paced back and forth. His path covered about 200 yards, ending halfway up a distant ridge. I tried every call I knew. The gobbler answered them, but he would not cross the creek. Even if he did, he would then have to cross a fence. According to every turkey hunting article I've ever read about difficult gobblers, the odds of calling him across the creek were thin. If he defied those odds, the odds of calling him past the fence were hopeless.

I serenaded the gobbler with three box calls and four slate calls using four different strikers. I used the finger yelpers and two mouth calls. Unable to coax the gobbler across the creek, I played my last card. I scratched a gobble on a dual-slotted cedar box made by my friend Bill Rhodes. The gobbler planted himself directly across the creek. I made contented hen clucks and purrs with a slate and diaphragm, following them with the box-call gobble. The tom gobbled furiously at the sound of a hen pillow-talking to another gobbler.

Hearing the commotion, Stanley texted to say he was parked under the cedar tree where my morning began.

"If he comes over, one of us will kill him," Stanley texted.

Finally, the gobbler's tone changed. It was no longer angry or demanding.

"I call this the plaintive gobble," Stanley texted. "He is in the crossing area. He just hasn't figured out how to get here yet."

Then, Stanley texted to say he had moved to a better ambush point about 150 yards west.

"I haven't called yet," he texted. "I want him to go to you."

And then it got quiet and stayed quiet.

"I think he gave us the slip," I texted.

"He never came over that I'm aware of," Stanley replied.

Shortly after, a dark shape materialized from the tall grass. About ninety yards away, a gobbler strode purposefully across the middle of the field. By gosh, he had done the impossible. He crossed the creek and the fence!

"And they say it can't be done!" I texted Stanley.

"Those gobblers don't read the same magazines that we do," Stanley replied.

I stopped the gobbler by striking a long purr on an aluminum slate. Only then did the tom seem to notice the decoy. I purred again. The tom gobbled twice and faced the decoy. Like popping open an umbrella, he spread his fan and closed the distance in full strut, plumage shimmering in the bright afternoon sunlight. His head glowed brilliant shades of white and blue. His red wattles were aflame. He pranced a few steps to the right, swung his fan around, and pranced a few steps to the left, relentlessly drawing nearer. Because of the woody shield in front of me and the broken woody wall behind me, the gobbler did not see the camo-clad figure in the void raise his gun.

At about 1:10 p.m., my Winchester put him down at twenty yards. I ran to the gobbler and knelt as I gasped a prayer of gratitude. This one was different from all the others. It was a tearful outpouring of relief after so much futility and also an affirmation of faith confirmed in such a miraculous ending. There were many other things I could have been doing that morning, but at their finest, none could have come remotely close to rivaling this.

The gobbler's bottlebrush beard was ten inches long. His spurs were only a half-inch long, but he weighed about twenty pounds.

Smoothing his feathers, I lifted my head at an owl hoot from the top of the hill. It was Stanley, arms raised triumphantly.

"I watched it all through binoculars from four-hundred yards away!" Stanley said when he reached me. "Man, what a display! I was texting play-by-play to Micaiah the whole time. Congratulations, brother. You earned this one!"

"Take a good long look at this bird, Brother Mike," I said. "This is a far cry from Woody. He's my diploma for all the things you've taught me. He's as much yours as he is mine."

"You're very kind, brother, but I can't take any credit for this one," Stanley said, shaking his head emphatically. "Patience killed this bird, the kind of patience I don't have. I wish I could hunt like you do, but my back won't let me. There were a lot of different ways this could have ended the wrong way, but you were flawless. I tip my hat to you."

Back at the lodge, we positioned the gobbler on a log and shot a short video recapping the hunt for the digital edition of the *Arkansas Democrat-Gazette*. Respecting coronavirus social distancing protocols, we wore masks, which not only looked silly but also muffled our voices so that we sounded like the unintelligible teacher in old Charlie Brown television cartoons. As we wrapped up the video, we started to extend our hands for a celebratory shake, but we remembered our coronavirus manners and touched elbows instead.

"Corona!" I shouted.

Stanley dubbed the bird, "Corona Carl."

That night at the lodge, after Stanley and I polished off a couple of big rib eye steaks, I arrayed all my calls on a long table. In addition to the three boxes I used to seduce Corona Carl, I had six other boxes that didn't make the day's starting lineup. Stanley handled them all, but his touch lingered on a Bill Rhodes cedar box.

"That's the one that sealed the deal on Corona Carl," I said.

Stanley held it near his ear and touched off a few yelps.

"Ooooh, that sounds sweet!" Stanley said.

"It's yours," I said.

Stanley's eyes widened. "Oh, no, sir! I'm not going to take a call away from you that you called up a gobbler with," he said.

"You're not taking it from me. I'm giving it to you" I said. "Would you rather have the call or a Gatorade shower? Your choice, Coach!"

Stanley smiled broadly.

"This one will stay in my truck, and I'll do it proud," he said.

Stanley was true to his word. On April 26, 2021, Stanley started his morning under the same cedar tree where my hunt for Corona Carl started one day shy of a year before. Prodded by inactivity, he crept down to the spoil pile and placed two decoys in the same spot where I put mine. A flock of jakes gobbled out of sight, but Stanley perked at the sound of a distant gobble.

"I'm not used to hunting turkeys from a stationary position," Stanley wrote in a text after the hunt. "When I heard the distant gobble of the bird I eventually killed, I badly wanted to go toward him, but I elected to stay put and ride it out like you did."

The game went from one of positioning to one of calling, but Stanley was prepared.

"I strung multiple calls around me and struck up a 'Bryan Hendricks turkey band' to keep me and the jakes entertained," Stanley texted. One of the calls was the Rhodes cedar box.

Stanley's music summoned the jakes, which frolicked around the decoys like adolescent boys at a prom trying to muster the nerve to ask the girls to dance. Finally, the big gobbler thundered from the field edge before it and two other adult gobblers charged and dispersed the jakes.

"It was like a jailbreak. I swear, one almost tripped on his beard, he was running so hard," Stanley texted.

Stanley was shooting video of the jakes with his phone when the gobblers appeared. He slid his phone into his pocket but forgot to turn it off. He texted me the video. I heard Stanley click off his shotgun's safety, followed by three quick yelps and a shotgun blast.

The gobbler, a bona fide Ozark trophy, had two long beards and long, needle-like spurs.

"I owe YOU an assist on that one," Stanley texted.

Teacher and pupil were now peers. The circle had closed.

the end